Overcoming life's difficulties

OVERCOMING LIFE'S DIFFICULTIES

Learning from the book of Joshua

Peter Jeffery

EVANGELICAL PRESS

EVANGELICAL PRESS
Faverdale North Industrial Estate, Darlington, DL3 0PH, England

Evangelical Press USA
P. O. Box 84, Auburn, MA 01501, USA

e-mail: sales@evangelical-press.org

web: www.evangelical-press.org

First published 1999

British Library Cataloguing in Publication Data available

ISBN 0 85234 434 1

Printed and bound in Great Britain by Creative Print & Design Wales,
Ebbw Vale

Contents

Introduction

Most Christians understand that many of the books of the New Testament were written for a particular purpose and that in general each deals primarily with a subject that was relevant to God's people at that time. So Romans presents the great doctrine of justification by faith; Galatians deals with a heresy that threatened the heart of the gospel; Corinthians grapples with serious problems in that church. All these first-century subjects continue to be crucial for the church of today. Very little of importance changes, so the teaching of the New Testament is always relevant. But what is true of the New Testament writings is also true of many of the books of the Old Testament. Principles and patterns are set before us that are as crucial for our day as they were in the time of Moses or David.

The book of Joshua deals with God's people entering the promised land. Canaan was the inheritance which the Lord promised Israel and many Christians have regarded it as a picture or type of heaven to which the church is travelling through the wilderness of this world. We find this in many hymns, where crossing the Jordan is equated with death and entering the promised land of heaven. But Canaan was the scene of many fierce battles — hardly a picture of heaven. What Canaan does strikingly and accurately foreshadow is what Christians will inevitably experience here and now in this world before they enter into heaven. The world is a battlefield for the Christian and God never promised us a trouble-free passage, but he does give us promises of help and strength that should encourage us to press on. This is the most important lesson we can learn from the book of Joshua.

Balance

If our concept of the Christian life is unbalanced then we shall have difficulty in applying the contents of Joshua to our times and our lives. To think of salvation and its effects only in terms of God's sovereign gift, and neglect all that Scripture says about human responsibility, will make it difficult to understand how, on the one hand, the land of Canaan was God's free gift to his people and yet, on the other, they were to fight hard and long to take possession of the gift. But that is exactly the pattern of the Christian life that the New Testament sets before us. Eternal life is both the gift of God (Rom. 6:23) and a crown that requires faithfulness on our part if we are to possess it (Rev. 2:10).

Salvation is by grace alone, and human merit has no place in it. Good works are not the means of salvation, but they are the inevitable fruit of a life in which grace is at work (Eph. 1:4). And living for God in an alien world will arouse the same sort of opposition that Joshua faced in the promised land. We do not battle to achieve God's favour, but because we are already God's people and because the world, which has always been against the Lord and his children, is clearly no friend of the believer who wishes to live his life for the glory of God.

During 1941 London was bombed night after night by German planes. This bombing was known as the Blitz. Thousands were killed and whole areas of the city completely destroyed. It was a frightening time to live in England's capital city. Yet only 200 miles away in Paris no bombs were falling. Why was London being blitzed and Paris not? The simple answer is that Hitler and his German army had already captured Paris. The French capital was no threat to them, hence no bombs. But London was a free city and very much opposed to Hitler. London was blitzed because it was at war with Germany.

The Christian is at war with Satan and all the power of evil, so it is not surprising that he bombards us with every type of temptation and trouble. These are evidence of the war and proof that we no longer belong to the devil.

What is taught historically in Joshua is also taught doctrinally in Hebrews: 'Now we who have believed enter that rest' (Heb. 4:3). The moment we are saved by the grace of God, heaven is guaranteed for us, but we do not enjoy it there and then.

Our place in heaven is as secure as that of those who are already there, and this truth brings comfort and assurance to us. But the experience of the truth is that, as well as comfort, we also become more conscious of sin, both in our hearts and in the world. Sin bothers us in a way it never did before. This spiritual sensitivity brings us into conflict with the world, the flesh and the devil. So Hebrews 4:11 calls upon us to 'make every effort to enter that rest'. Effort, labouring, striving — this is the language the New Testament uses to show what is required of us if we are to enjoy the promises of God. Paul says, 'I have fought the good fight, I have finished the race, I have kept the faith. Now there is in store for me the crown of righteousness, which the Lord, the righteous Judge, will award to me on that day — and not only to me, but also to all who have longed for his appearing' (2 Tim. 4:7-8).

Lessons

As well as the points we have already made, the book of Joshua teaches us some basic lessons that we greatly need to learn and apply to our lives today.

1. The prevailing one-sided evangelicalism of today emphasizes an easy-believism and a cosy gospel. It tells sinners all they need to do is to believe in Jesus and every problem will go away. A better marriage, a more prosperous job, a bigger house will all be theirs. The incentive to become a Christian is not that I am a hell-deserving sinner who needs salvation, but instead is taken straight out of the world's materialistic philosophy. It is true that there are unbelievable blessings in Christ, but they are spiritual, not material. There is also a fight to be fought and a race to be won before we enter heaven's gates.

2. There is a miserable and unbiblical view amongst some believers that this life is one constant battle and defeat. Victory rarely enters either their vocabulary or their experience, and they portray the Christian life as one misery after another. Joshua shows us that victory is God's will for his people, but the Lord lays down the conditions on which the victory is achieved. Paul clearly believed this and was confident that he could do all things in and through the grace and power of the Lord Jesus Christ. The same truth is applicable for us today and we should be knowing more victory in our spiritual lives. The book of Joshua can help us to this end.

3. Canaan was never fully conquered by Joshua's army, but bit by bit they enjoyed what the Lord had promised them. In the same way there are for us present spiritual conquests and blessings that are ours to obtain and enjoy. The promise of Isaiah 64:4 and 1 Corinthians 2:9:

No eye has seen,
  no ear has heard,
no mind has conceived
  what God has prepared for those who love him,

is not speaking of future blessings in heaven that can only be
imagined, but of things that God has already revealed by his
Spirit. In other words, there is so much more to know and
experience of God here and now.

1.
Blessings don't come easily

Joshua 1:1-5

The death of Moses was a great loss to the Israelites. For many years they had depended upon him as their leader. During his lifetime Moses had received more than his fair share of criticism and his advice was not always appreciated. This very often is the cost of leadership. In spite of this the people valued this exceptional man and they felt his death deeply: 'The Israelites grieved for Moses in the plains of Moab thirty days' (Deut. 34:8). Calvin says, 'The people were like a body with its head lopped off.'[1]

There is no doubt that, by any standard, Moses was a remarkable man. The tribute paid him in Deuteronomy 34:10 is glowing: 'Since then, no prophet has risen in Israel like Moses, whom the LORD knew face to face.' Like all believers, Moses had his spiritual ups and downs, but the main characteristic of his life was submission to the will of God. This characteristic was required of the new leader and, as we shall see, of all God's people.

The death of this great man did not mean the end of God's work among the Israelites. We too often tend to link the work of God with particular men and think that if the man dies or moves on the work will fizzle out. Sometimes, sadly, this is true, but that does not have to be the case. We need to learn that God's work is not hindered by the death of his servants, no matter how great a blessing they have been to us. Matthew Henry says, 'God will change hands to show that whatever instruments he uses, he is not tied to any.'[2]

The church is to value its spiritual leaders highly, but the work is God's, not man's. Sooner or later the man will go, and if our eye is too much on him, and not on the Lord, our faith and spiritual expectations will suffer. The more the Lord has used the man to bless our souls, the more prone we are to put him on a pedestal, but if his ministry has been biblical and Christ-centred we shall soon come to appreciate that the man was only the channel by which God's blessing came to us and we shall look expectantly for the Lord to provide a new leader.

In this case the new leader was Joshua but, because the work was God's, this did not mean that there was to be a completely new message for the people. The message remained the same but Joshua was to introduce a new sphere of activity: 'Now then, you and all these people, get ready to cross the Jordan River into the land I am about to give to them' (1:2). The command was not to Joshua as an individual, but as the new leader of the people. He was to lead them into the fulfilment of the promise God had made to Abraham centuries before. All that Moses did was leading up to this. It was crucial, necessary, but preliminary, and now Joshua had the great responsibility of leading the nation into the promised land.

God's gift and command

The opening verses of Joshua emphasize that the promised land was God's gift to his people. They were not entitled to it. Neither they nor their ancestors had done anything to merit it. Neither would the blood and sacrifice of the ensuing battles warrant any idea that they had earned it. It was God's gift. Nevertheless they would not enter into possession of it without great effort. God required their obedience, and this meant that a very real responsibility was placed upon them. The land was God's gift, but they had to fight for every inch of it. This is a prime lesson from the book of Joshua that we must learn for the health of our own spiritual lives.

Canaan was first promised to Abraham; he is the father of all who believe (Rom. 4:11) and so he is a model, or pattern, for our faith. His example to us is that of faith and obedience because this is how we receive God's promise. It is interesting that on the first occasion when God mentions Canaan to Abraham he does not speak of the land as a gift: 'Leave your country ... and go to the land I will *show* you' (Gen. 12:1). It is much later that God talks about *giving* him the land. In other words, Abraham was first required to break completely with his old life and to trust and obey God before any promise was made to him. The call of God put costly and definite demands upon Abraham. This was no easy pilgrimage or soft option, but one that involved sacrifice, commitment and trust.

If Abraham is the father of all who believe, it is not surprising that every Christian is called upon to walk the same path. We too are to live by faith and obedience because a saving faith does not just major on God's promises but, first, it takes very seriously the divine commands. Faith and obedience are crucial to the Christian life because Christ is the source of salvation to all who obey him (Heb. 5:9). Faith and obedience are inseparable twins. Where there is one, inevitably there will be the other, so Paul speaks in Romans 1:5 of 'the obedience that comes from faith'.

On the banks of the Jordan, with Moses dead, Joshua, the new leader who like Moses was a descendant of Abraham, was called upon to act with a similar faith and to trust God and obey him. Jordan was to be crossed and when that had been done there would be enemies to confront. There would be no avoiding battles or sacrifice as long as the people were obedient to God. All this must be done before Israel could enjoy the inheritance God had given them.

God's promise

The prospect must have been daunting to Joshua but he was encouraged with the promise: 'I will give you every place where you set your foot, as I promised Moses' (1:3). God required that Israel was to be obedient, but the guarantee of victory would not be the result of this, but of God's promise and God's working on their behalf. God would give victory, not as a matter of course, but only as Israel yielded to his authority and obeyed his word. So we come back again to this basic principle that Canaan was the free gift of God to his people, but they would only obtain the fulness and blessing of the gift by their own effort.

There is nothing contradictory about this because the same is still true. Salvation is the gift of God. We do nothing to earn or merit it, but if we are to enjoy it fully now and receive all its promised blessings, then there are battles to be fought and a victory to be won. The only way to fight these battles is by obedience to God's will. Obedience will always enrich the Christian's life, so inevitably the miserable, unhappy, complaining believer is always the disobedient believer. Obedience to God's will never makes a Christian unhappy. It may make him uncomfortable for a while, but in the end it will lead to joy and peace.

The command of Joshua 1:2, 'Get ready to cross the Jordan,' is followed by the promise of verses 3-5: 'I will give you every place where you set your foot... No one will be able to stand up against you all the days of your life. As I was with Moses, so I will be with you; I will never leave you nor forsake you.' These verses teach us much about the spiritual battles we are to fight. There is so much blessing for us in Christ, but it does not come easily. There are enemies who would seek to prevent us from enjoying all that God has for us. We have to fight, but we do so knowing that in Christ we are certain to win. However, verse 3 reminds us that the victory is one step at a time.

There may be some Christians who object that being victors in Christ sounds great, but it is not working for them. All they seem to experience is one defeat after another. One reason for this may be a lack of trust in God. There are many believers who want everything tied up neatly and tidily before they will do anything. Unlike Peter on the Sea of Galilee (Matt. 14:28-31), they would never even get out of the boat. It is easy to criticize Peter for becoming fearful, but at least he had the faith to trust Jesus and get out of the boat and walk on the water. Another reason is the failure to realize that God does not give us all the victory after one battle. We remember God's promise in Exodus 23:29-30: 'But I will not drive them out in a single year, because the land would become desolate and the wild animals too numerous for you. Little by little I will drive them out before you, until you have increased enough to take possession of the land.' We need to remember the words, 'little by little'.

Why did the Lord not deal with the Canaanites before Israel arrived? Why did they have to fight? Why does God not make it impossible for us to sin? Why do we have to face the continuous struggle against the world, the flesh and the devil? There are many answers to these questions and one is that 'little by little' keeps us in a state of constant dependence upon God. The battles are not so much to defeat the enemy, but to deal with our arrogance and self-confidence and to teach us more and more to lean upon the Lord.

God never promises us complete victory over sin all at once; therefore we should not be surprised by the battles. If Israel was not to be discouraged by their slow progress in the promised land, neither must we be discouraged if victory is not ours at once. We must not think that slowness means that victory will never come. Growth in grace is not instantaneous, like new birth; it is gradual and takes time. This is not to encourage spiritual indifference and laziness. Our business is to get into the battle, to fight and obey and trust the Lord for victory. It may be little by little but it is sure: 'No one will be able to stand up against you all the days of your life. As I was with Moses, so I will be with you; I will never leave you nor forsake you' (1:5).

2.
Focusing on God

Joshua 1:5-9

Joshua had been second in command to Moses for some time, so he would have known that in all probability he would one day succeed the great man, but when it happened he must have been overwhelmed by doubts. Two things would have been uppermost in his mind, the first of which was the awesome responsibility of following a man of the calibre of Moses. God has given spiritual giants to his church from time to time and they have been a source of great blessing, but they can also appear to be in a different league from the rest of us. We see them at their peak and, compared with them, we feel like pygmies. But we forget that they were not always like that. Moses at the beginning of his ministry was fearful and uncertain. He became what he was only because of God's grace. Joshua's hope of being a great leader was not to lie in any natural abilities he may have had, but in the confidence that God was with him. So he needed the promise of verse 5: 'As I was with Moses, so I will be with you, I will never leave you nor forsake you.'

Secondly, Joshua might have thought that it was not a good time for Israel to change leaders. A crucial moment had arrived for God's people and he probably thought that they needed Moses now more than ever. There was a land to conquer and enemies to subdue. The immediate future was going to be difficult enough without having the added burden of a new leader. So again the promise of Joshua 1:5 came as a great encouragement: 'No one will be able to stand up against you all the days of your life.'

A promise given

Moses had used almost the same words in encouraging the people (Deut. 7:24). God's people would be victorious, and that promise is as valid today as it was then. In Romans Paul relates Abraham's experience of God to the believers of his day: 'The words "it was credited to him" were written not for him alone, but also for us, to whom God will credit righteousness — for us who believe in him who raised Jesus our Lord from the dead' (Rom. 4:23-24).

The value of a promise does not lie in the thing promised but in the one who makes it. What Abraham Lincoln promised his people, or Napoleon promised the people of France in his day, will not be of much encouragement to us today. The men who made those promises are dead and their promises died with them. But the one who makes the promises of Scripture is the eternal and everlasting God. The unchanging God, whose purpose for this world is exactly the same as it was in Joshua's day, still says to us, 'As I was with Moses, so I will be with you; I will never leave you nor forsake you.' The divine promises, made on particular occasions to various individuals, are of general value to all believers of all ages. The same promise is made to a Christian church in Hebrews 13:5-6:

God has said,

'Never will I leave you,
    never will I forsake you.'

So we say with confidence,

'The Lord is my helper; I will not be afraid.
    What can man do to me?'

This is the confidence we can have in God when we are seeking to follow him and fight his battles.

These encouragements tell us what they were meant to tell Joshua: 'Take your eyes off the problems and focus on the grace and power of God.' When we do that God will not disappoint us.

There is a great example of this in 2 Chronicles 20. King Jehoshaphat was told that a huge enemy army was coming against him. Jehoshaphat was no fool and his first reaction to the news was alarm. He knew he had no military resources to deal with the situation, so quite naturally he was fearful. But he did not stay like that because, as we are told, he prayed to the Lord. His prayer centres on the power of God: 'Power and might are in your hand, and no one can withstand you.' He acknowledges his weakness and ends the prayer by confessing, 'For we have no power to face this vast army that is attacking us. We do not know what to do, but our eyes are upon you' (2 Chr. 20:6,12). God's answer was: 'Do not be afraid or discouraged because of this vast army. For the battle is not yours but God's' (2 Chr. 20:15).

Jehoshaphat's God was Joshua's God, and he is also our God.

An obligation imposed

The promise of verse 5 was an assurance of ultimate victory, but it was not an incentive for Joshua to take it easy, as if there was nothing for him to do. The promise was an encouragement to action and duty because God immediately put certain obligations upon his servant. Joshua was to 'be strong and courageous', and to be obedient to the commands of God. God's promises do not annul his commands. The Christian who argues that, because God has promised never to leave us or forsake us and our salvation is eternally secure, therefore it is safe to play around with sin, has never understood God or salvation. Thank God for the promise; it is great to know that we shall never lose our salvation, but God never encourages sin, and the promise is intended to inspire confidence for effort and commitment, not carelessness. A. W. Pink says, 'If our response to God's promises be that of sloth and carelessness, that is proof we have received them carnally and not spiritually. The use or misuse we make of the divine cordials affords a good index to the state of our hearts.'[1]

Joshua knew that God would pardon sin but that he would never excuse or tolerate it. And sin in a Christian robs him of blessing. Moses never entered the promised land because of what happened at Meribah Kadesh (Deut. 32:51-52). Divine commands must be taken seriously and, while we rejoice in the promises, we need to be careful to meet our obligations.

The effect of the promise on Joshua should be to create strength and courage in him. The task facing him was enough to make the strongest heart tremble; nevertheless he was to do it without hesitation because the living God had promised him victory. Joshua had every reason to be strong and courageous.

Strength and courage are what Christians need today if we are to overcome our spiritual enemies and enjoy all that God has for us. These qualities are not natural endowments that we may be born with. Many believers are by nature anything but courageous. They fear ridicule, fear their opponents and fear each other. So we see a promise like verse 5 and argue that it is easier said than done. Our problem is that we fail to mix faith with the promises of God. What more can we want than the assurance that God will never leave us or forsake us? Our strength is not to be derived from any natural abilities we may have, and our courage not from a confidence in our own ability. Our hope must be in the Lord, who guarantees us victory when we unreservedly trust him. We are to meet our God-given obligations by being obedient and courageous. That is not unreasonable and it should not be too hard for someone who has already been saved by divine grace.

In verse 7 God repeats the command to be strong and courageous, only this time it is very definitely linked to the specific duty of obedience. It takes courage to be obedient to God's Word. A life that is lived in submission to God will be out of step with the rest of the world and will therefore inevitably be misunderstood and scorned. To be called old-fashioned and narrow-minded is not pleasant. To lose friends and the respect of others can be costly; some believers are not prepared to pay the cost. Is not one of the main reasons for our disobedience to God that we are afraid to be too different from the world? But very clearly we are not to be regulated by our own inclinations. We are not to be governed by expediency or popular opinion. For the believer all that should matter is: 'What does God say?' Such obedience is the result, not only of believing the promises of God, but also of a real awareness of God in our hearts.

Joshua would require strength and courage to be obedient because what was involved was no brief, five-minute experience, but years of persevering effort. Canaan was not conquered after one battle. It was a task that was to take the rest of Joshua's life. There was to be no letting up. There would be victories to rejoice in, but also defeats to despair over. Is this not a vivid picture of the Christian life? It is warfare from beginning to end. When victory has been won over one sin, another rears its ugly head. Temptation is never far away and the believer is always in the minority. Something more than human strength is called for. If this is the case, why bother? Because we are God's people and this is the way we have to go. The way is narrow and hard, but blessings are given daily, not only to encourage endurance, but for us to enjoy and delight in our God. This, says verses 7 and 8, is the path to success and prosperity. This does not mean plenty of money, but something far better — peace with God, joy in assurance, a hope of glory and an inheritance we cannot lose.

The path of obedience is the path of blessing. It will attract the frowns of men, but what does that matter if we have the smile of God? Even in the midst of difficulties it is a joy to know that it is better to be in the battle than in the slavery of sin.

3.
Knowing God's will

Joshua 1:7-8

The question of knowing what God wants us to do has always been a difficult one for Christians. Guidance is never easy but we know how crucial it is. Self-interest, fanciful theories, misguided enthusiasm and many other things can lead us astray and we need a more certain light to walk by. Joshua must have felt this keenly when he took over leadership of God's people. Abraham and Moses had each received instruction from God by the direct spoken word. To a certain extent Joshua was to experience the same thing, but now God gives him something Abraham and Moses never had. Joshua was to be under the authority of a written word. Here was his guide. Here was the Word of God for his people. We too are to be governed by the Book.

The task facing Joshua was enormous and he had every reason to be terrified and discouraged, but God urges him not to feel like this because he could be assured of the divine presence. But this presence was not to be taken as an opportunity for complacency and indolence. God's blessing was dependent upon Joshua's obedience to God's will as revealed in the 'Book of the Law' (1:8).

The book referred to was the law Moses had written down and given to Joshua. Over the years Moses had kept a written record of God's dealings with him (Deut. 31:9). Before he died Moses had finished writing everything God wanted in the book up to this point (Deut. 31:24). The authority of the book did not depend upon its size. The book commended to Joshua would have been what we know as the first five books of the Bible. This is called in Scripture the Law of Moses. There are other references to 'the Law of Moses and the Prophets' — which clearly included far more than just the writings of Moses. The phrase that Jesus used in describing God's book was 'the Law, the Prophets and the Psalms', which is what we know as the Old Testament.

These are all descriptions of the same book — growing in size and becoming more varied in content as, slowly, over the centuries, God revealed his will to his people, but never varying in its authority. The whole Bible took about 1400 years to be completed but at every stage of its development it is the Book of God.

The place of the Book

Clearly, in Joshua 1, and in every reference to the written Word of God in Scripture, the place of the Book is to be a place of authority. This authority is not to be regulated by situation or experience. Rather, the experiences that Joshua was to face were to be interpreted and faced in the light of 'everything written in' the Book of the Law. Our situation is no different. We too are under the authority of the Word of God. To some this may appear to be restrictive. Surely a book written centuries ago cannot be relevant to present situations? Moses at the Red Sea was in a totally different situation from Joshua facing the walls of Jericho, and even more different from a Christian facing the twenty-first century and under pressure in a factory. But this is no ordinary book. It is not merely the experiences and opinions of Moses; it is God's Word — eternal, unchanging and always relevant.

Joshua was told to 'be *careful* to do everything written in it'. In other words, he was not to be casual or flippant in his attitude towards the Book. He was to take care in working out the demands of God's law because, with all the authority Joshua had as leader of the people, he himself was still to be subject to the Book. This book is God's book and if we are God's people it is to be part of us, so that we can say with Martin Luther, 'My conscience is subject to the Word of God', and with John Wesley, 'At any price give me the Book of God. Let me be the man of one book.'

The question of authority has always been fundamental for Christianity. Particularly throughout this twentieth century, the authority of the Bible has been challenged. But, as Dr Lloyd-Jones wrote, 'The choice for us today is really as simple as it was for those first Christians in the early days. We either accept this authority or else we accept the authority of modern knowledge, modern science, human understanding, human ability. It is one or the other. Let us not be confused by the modern argument about a changed position. We are still left where believers have always been left. It is still Christ or the critics.'[1]

The purpose of the Book

When Christians show a love and regard for the Bible they are often accused of Bible worship. The accusation is totally false because it is not the book as a collection of pages and print that we love, but the God who gave us this remarkable revelation, who inspired it; and we love particularly the Lord Jesus Christ who is revealed to us in its pages. In India there are some Hindus who have a copy of the Bible in their temple. They keep it in a brass box and every now and again bring it out and worship it. They have no knowledge of the God of the Bible and make no effort to understand or obey the teaching of the Bible; they simply have a book that they worship. That is Bible worship and it is totally different from how a Christian regards the Word of God.

The Christian sees that the purpose of the Bible is to reveal God to him, and he is to meditate on God's Word and obey it. This is what Joshua was told was to be his attitude to the Book, and it is what the New Testament encourages in us. A superficial attitude to the Bible is to be avoided. Love for God himself is defined in terms of obeying the commands of God (1 John 5:3).

Meditation upon the Word of God is one of the most valuable blessings open to the believer, and it is essential for spiritual growth. Meditation means more than just reading the Bible; it is giving time to the Scriptures, and this means taking time from something else. It is a matter of priorities. Meditation is what Psalm 23 is referring to when it talks about lying down in green pastures. It is the lying down of the soul, the chewing over and digesting of the green pastures. Without this you can stand in the most lush spiritual pastures and be spiritually undernourished. Therefore this is not optional, only to be done when we feel like it, but a daily obligation for all Christians. The command Joshua received to meditate day and night is applicable to us all because this is set before us over and over again in Scripture (Ps. 48:9; 119:15; 143:5).

Meditation in God's law day and night is one of the outstanding marks of the man whom Psalm 1 calls 'blessed'. But though it is a command and of obvious spiritual benefit, how many of us actually do it? Our usual excuse is that we are too busy. Our lives are so crowded with duties and responsibilities that we have no time for quiet meditation and study of God's

Word. We satisfy ourselves with reading a daily Bible portion. This is good but it is not enough and meditation is far more than that. It is to read, pray, think, consider and ponder.

Meditation is vital to the well-being of our souls, so we can be sure that God never calls us to a lifestyle that crowds out the spiritual essentials. Christ's yoke is easy and his burden is light, so if our burden is too heavy then it is self-imposed. The call of God is for us to set our affections on things above. When we plead that we are too busy to meditate we are simply not facing up to the biblical teaching that 'Where your treasure is, there your heart will be also.' Is it not true that we can usually find time for the things we enjoy? The psalmist could say, 'Oh, how I love your law! I meditate on it all day long' (Ps. 119:97). To him meditation was a joy; so he found time for it.

There is no doubt that for many Christians life is very busy; they have their job, their families and their church responsibilities; but Matthew Henry, commenting on Joshua said, 'If ever any man's business might have excused him from meditation, and other acts of devotion, one would think Joshua's might at this time; it was a great trust that was lodged in his hands; the care of it was enough to fill him, if he had ten souls, and yet he must find time and thoughts for meditation. Whatever affairs of this world we have to mind, we must not neglect the one thing needful.'[2]

Meditation is not an end in itself. It should and must lead to obedience. It is easy to persuade ourselves that we want to live our lives in a way that pleases God, but how honest is this? If we really want to be obedient Christians then we must set ourselves to knowing what God's will is. That means knowing the Scriptures, because ignorance of God's ways makes it impossible to do the things that please him. One of God's chief complaints against Israel was:

I reared children and brought them up,
   but they have rebelled against me

                                          (Isa. 1:2).

The next verse tells us why this rebellion took place:

The ox knows his master,
   the donkey his owner's manger,
but Israel does not know,
   my people do not understand.

Ignorance was the product of lack of understanding, and for a child of God this is always the result of not using the capacity God has given us all to know his will and purposes.

Christians today seem to be obsessed with wanting blessings. But blessing, as Joshua is reminded, is the fruit of obedience. We can do what we like and say what we like, but until we give time to meditating on the things of God, and then obey what we see in the Book, we shall never know real blessing. This was the challenge to Joshua and it is always the same challenge that Christians have to face in every generation.

4.
God expects total obedience

Joshua 1:10-18

God had given Joshua his orders and also encouraged him with the twin promises of the divine presence and the divine blessing. Joshua knew that the Lord expected from him a total obedience. There were two things that needed to be done. One was the immediate task of crossing the River Jordan; the other was the long-term battle to conquer the land. The former might have seemed rather mundane compared with the glamour and adventure of conquest, but there could be no conquest until the first hurdle of crossing the Jordan was behind them. As Christians we must appreciate that in the work of God there are no little commands or big commands. Every command of God is crucial to the ultimate outcome. Even what we might consider to be the relatively easy things that the Lord commands us to do will be impossible without his help. Joshua was to discover this when the Israelites tried to cross the River Jordan.

No delay

The Scriptures teach that the believer's next move after hearing God speak is always prompt obedience without delay. The psalmist said, 'I will hasten and not delay to obey your

commands' (Ps. 119:60). This is exactly what Joshua did. God
spoke, so immediately Joshua set the wheels in motion for the
whole nation to obey. It is no use giving lip-service to obedience if we delay doing God's will. Delay is nearly always a
result of lack of heart for the matter. We are told in Nehemiah
that the rebuilding of the walls in Jerusalem proceeded at a
remarkable pace and the reason was that the people enthusiastically entered into the labour. Once duty is known it ought
to be done.

Joshua did not waste time grumbling about the difficulties
or inventing excuses to do nothing. He got on with the business because he believed and trusted God and had a heart that
loved to obey God. Paul commands us, 'Whatever you do,
work at it with all your heart, as working for the Lord, not for
men' (Col. 3:23). Where there is no heart there will be delay.
It is inevitable, and what is also inevitable is that by delay we
lose the blessings of obedience.

Another reason for delay is a fear of doing the wrong thing.
This in turn is a product of uncertainty as to what exactly God
requires of us. It may be true that in some areas of guidance
there can be uncertainty, and then delay would be prudent, but
in most areas of church life uncertainty is not a product of
ignorance but of a heart out of touch with God. The commands of God as to personal holiness, love for each other and
evangelism are so clear in Scripture that a reluctance to obey
them can only stem from an unwilling spirit.

When Joshua met with his officers (1:10) it was not to con-
fer with them on what was the best thing to do. He was not
having a committee meeting. There are times when consul-
tation is a must, but not when God had so clearly spoken.[1]
This was not the first time Joshua had spoken with conviction
and confidence to the nation, encouraging them to cross the
Jordan. He had done so forty years previously (Num. 14:6-9),
but the response of the people then had been a threat to stone

him. Those people were now dead and Joshua speaks here to
their descendants. The older generation had paid a terrible price
for their disobedience. Wiersbe makes the telling statement:
'The older we get, the more danger there is that we get set in
our ways and become "sanctified obstructionists"; but it doesn't
have to happen. Caleb and Joshua were the oldest men in the
camp, and yet they were enthusiastic about trusting God and
entering the land. It isn't a matter of age; it's a matter of faith;
and faith comes from meditating on the Word of God.'[2]

The words of Joshua in verse 11 are full of confidence and
practicality. 'Get your supplies ready,' he says. Trusting God
does not mean indolence and inactivity. If God did not say,
'Prepare boats,' he did say, 'Prepare food.' A long journey lay
ahead, battles were to be fought and an army marches on its
stomach. God never encourages laziness and the doctrines of
the sovereignty of God and divine providence are no excuse
for spiritual or practical slothfulness. It is hypocrisy to claim
for ourselves the promises of Joshua 1:5,9, and to disregard
the command of verse 8 to be careful to do everything written
in the Book of the Law.

United for battle

There was another matter of great importance that Joshua had
to sort out before the battles for the promised land started.
Moses had come to an agreement with the Reubenites, Gadites
and the half-tribe of Manasseh. These people owned a great
deal of cattle and they saw that the land on the east of the
Jordan was ideal cattle country. So they asked Moses, 'Let
this land be given to your servants as our possession. Do not
make us cross the Jordan' (Num. 32:5). Moses was not at all
pleased with this. He called these tribes 'a brood of sinners'
(Num. 32:14). There were two fears in his mind: first, that the

request would bring God's anger upon the people; and, secondly, that they were avoiding their responsibility to fight for
the land with the rest of Israel.

The unity of the people was at stake and, more importantly,
Moses feared losing God's blessing and protection. The matter was sorted out when the two and a half tribes assured Moses
that their fighting men would cross the Jordan and take their
place with the rest of Israel in the coming battles. But Moses
was now dead and it was Joshua's duty to remind them of
their promise. It was more than a promise; it was an obligation and Joshua called upon them to fulfil it.

His concern was not that he could ill afford to lose the
manpower of these tribes. The battles would be won by trust
in God and not the size of the army. He insisted that they cross
the Jordan because they were God's people and none of the
Lord's people have the right to be at rest while their brethren
are fighting battles. These tribes had already received their
inheritance and there was nothing over Jordan for them. They
may have been tempted to argue that they could not leave
their families and possessions. Many excuses could have been
thought up to avoid keeping the promise. They made none
and the promise was honoured. At the end of the campaigns
Joshua paid them a glowing tribute: ' "For a long time now —
to this very day — you have not deserted your brothers but
have carried out the mission the LORD your God gave you…"
Then Joshua blessed them and sent them away, and they went
to their homes' (22:3,6).

This incident teaches us several basic lessons about the
Christian life. We need to share the concern of both Moses
and Joshua that nothing should be done to displease God. In
this case the fear was unfounded, but Moses' words, 'If you
turn away from following him, he will again leave all this people
in the desert, and you will be the cause of their destruction'
(Num. 32:15), show how deeply he felt the reality of the Lord's

anger. This sort of concern will seem very strange to many Christians today who see the Lord only as an easy-going and genial father-figure who exists to supply them with blessings on demand. But Moses had lived through forty terrible years in the desert under the judgement of God. He dreaded having to face that again, so his fear was understandable. The Lord is no temperamental prima donna, but he is a holy God who expects his people to take seriously his commands and to trust him wholeheartedly for direction and guidance. The fear of the Lord is not a cringing terror, but the wise and reasonable response of a heart that has enjoyed the mercies of God and dreads to offend this God who has demonstrated his love and concern for his people over and over again.

Moses also feared that the action of the two and a half tribes would discourage the Israelites (Num. 32:7). Once a man is saved he loses any right he thinks he may have to please himself. His prime concern must be to please the Lord, and following hard after this must be a concern for the welfare of his fellow believers. We cannot live for ourselves. Every action and word that originates in us will have an effect, for good or evil, on other Christians. Paul's testimonial of Philemon, 'Your love has given me great joy and encouragement, because you, brother, have refreshed the hearts of the saints,' ought to be something all believers should covet as being true of themselves. An excellent example of this is seen in Psalm 73. The psalmist was feeling spiritually low and in verses 2-14 we can see the state of his soul. But he did not go around proclaiming his miseries to all who would listen. He says in verse 15, 'If I had said, "I will speak thus," I would have betrayed your children.' Spurgeon says of this verse, 'From such a man as the psalmist, the utterance which his discontent suggested would have been a heavy blow and deep discouragement to the whole brotherhood... We ought to look at the consequences of our speech to all others, and especially to the church of God. Woe unto the man by whom offence cometh! Rash, undigested, ill-considered speech is respons-ible for much of the heart-burning and trouble in the churches.'[3]

Lastly, the words of Joshua, 'You are to help your brothers until the LORD gives them rest, as he has done for you' (1:15), reminds us that we are never to let our brethren stand alone. Their battles are ours, and when the Lord blesses us in any way, spiritually or materially, the biblical response is to ask, 'How can I best use this blessing to the glory of God, to the welfare of his people and to the building up of the church?' There is no room in Christianity for isolationism. We are one people and one church. So if one section of the church enjoys peace and prosperity, it is to use these blessings to stand along-side other Christians who may be in trouble. The problems of believers in Muslim lands where they are persecuted bitterly may not be ours in experience, but they ought to be ours in emotion, as we feel their needs and do all we can in prayer and other ways to help relieve their difficulties.

5.
Welcoming sinners

Joshua 2

When Joshua sent two spies to gain information about Jericho he had no idea that the Lord had prepared a place of safety for them in the pagan city. The prostitute Rahab was probably the last person they would have expected to help them, but she risked her life to protect them.

The problem is that this protection involved Rahab in lying to the King of Jericho's soldiers. In the circumstances confronting her, was she right in lying? Yes, says R. T. Kendall, she 'lied for the glory of God... Her faith also proved greater and more honourable than telling the truth — which would have been fatal to the two spies.'[1] No, says John Calvin, 'We must admit that though it was done for a good purpose, it was not free from fault. For those who hold what is called a dutiful lie to be altogether excusable, do not sufficiently consider how precious truth is in the sight of God.'[2]

Her lie

The ninth commandment says, 'You shall not give false testimony against your neighbour' — you shall not lie. That ought to settle the matter. Rahab was wrong. We know that her motives were right but that does not make a lie right. The

Roman Catholic Jesuits in the Inquisition would appeal to this action of Rahab to support their dogma that the end justifies the means. That was their excuse for burning Protestants at the stake. But the same sort of sentiment, 'Let us do evil that good may come,' is firmly rejected by Paul in Romans. It is argued that not all lies are covered by the ninth commandment. Circumstances make cases; so, for instance, is it so terrible to tell a dying man that he will recover from his illness? Is not this a kindness rather than a sin? So we talk of harmless white lies, and there is an element of truth in this reasoning, but none the less it is a very dangerous path for a Christian to walk. Who decides what is harmless and what is not?

Does any circumstance justify sin? And no one can doubt that lying is sin. In Rahab's circumstances it could be argued that she was forced either to tell a lie or to betray the spies, which meant that they would be killed. She was confronted with a dilemma in which she had to choose between the lesser of two evils and we would all have to sympathize with her. But surely that is an argument that takes no account of God. Had Rahab kept silent and refused to say anything, or had she even told the truth, was God unable to protect his servants? Do we believe that God needs a violation of his own laws to bring about his will and purpose?

We shall look next at Rahab's faith and see how the New Testament emphasizes this and ignores her lie. Is this because the New Testament writers recognized that the faith of this woman was still immature? She knew little of the ways of the Lord and acted according to the light she had. If we were honest, we would have to admit that in a similar situation we would probably have done the same thing. Warren Wiersbe says, 'Lying is wrong (Proverbs 12:22), and the fact that God had Rahab's lies recorded in Scripture is no proof that he approved of them. However, let's confess that most of us would hesitate to tell the truth *if it really were a matter of life and death.* It's one thing for *me* to tell the truth about myself and suffer for it; but do I have the right to cause the death of *others*, especially those who come under my roof for protection? Many people have been honoured for deceiving the enemy during war time and saving innocent lives, and this was war.'[3]

Without the restraining hand of God the strongest of us are mere weaklings, and therefore none of us is in any position to point a finger at Rahab, but neither is any justified in condoning her action. Rahab is not to be used as an excuse to lie. What we ought to do is pray that the Lord would keep us from such situations. We see in Scripture several situations in which we could be tempted to lie. Rahab lied to protect others. Peter, in the courtyard, lied to avoid trouble for himself. Ananias and Sapphira lied to impress others. We can sympathize with Rahab but there is no virtue whatsoever in the lies of the others. The hallmark of Christianity is truth and this is not to be diluted in any way.

Her faith

The outstanding feature of Rahab's faith is that it magnifies the riches of divine mercy. She belonged to a heathen race that was to be completely wiped out, yet God saved her. Not only that, but she personally was a notorious sinner, a prostitute, yet God had mercy on her. There was nothing in this woman's background or lifestyle to commend her to God, yet she was saved and given a place of honour in the family of God so that her great-great-grandson was King David.

There are indications in the story that God was working in Rahab before she met the spies. Her words in verse 9, 'I know that the LORD has given this land to you', are the language of faith. How did she know this? Like everyone else in Jericho, she had heard what God had done for his people (2:10-11).

They all heard and all believed the reports, but there was a marked difference in Rahab from the rest of the people. They were terrified and their hearts melted in fear, but that was all — there was no faith. They knew their fate was sealed, but there was no calling on God for mercy and grace. They still opposed God and would have killed his servants, even though that would not have changed the outcome. They feared, but they still continued in their sin.

Rahab also feared but she knew that God's will would be done at Jericho. The spies were welcomed because of this. She saw that her safety lay in protecting these two men, but the New Testament goes way beyond that. She was not just acting out of self-interest but 'By faith the prostitute Rahab, because she welcomed the spies, was not killed with those who were disobedient' (Heb. 11:31).

Her faith, like ours, was the gift of God. Consequently she heard the news about God not merely with an eye to self-protection, but with a vision of God's grace and promises being fulfilled. She wanted a part in all that God had for his people. It is clear from her statement that 'The LORD has given this land to you' (2:8), that Jericho had heard something about God's promise to Abraham. Rahab believed these promises. She saw that this God was not only all-powerful but also gracious and loving in the care of his people. She was saved not by fear, but by faith. It was because she believed God that she received the spies with faith, not because she saw an opportunity to save her own skin.

No one else in Jericho would have done what she did, even though they were all afraid. In receiving the spies with peace Rahab made it clear that she believed God. Her testimony at the end of verse 11, 'The LORD your God is God in heaven above and on the earth below,' is not an expression of fear but of faith. As a result she had a welcoming love for God's people and was ready to help them. It is true that there was much in

Rahab's faith that was weak and ignorant, but none the less her faith was real and the New Testament rejoices in it.

Her lifestyle

A true faith will always lead to repentance, and repentance will produce a new lifestyle because old things pass away and things inevitably change in the new life of a child of God. So if this woman had come to faith before she met the spies, did she continue as a prostitute? A. W. Pink argues that though she is called a prostitute she was not still following this lifestyle and the fact that she had stalks of flax laid out on the roof is proof that she was now an industrious, hard-working woman.[4] Whether this is true or mere speculation, what is certain is that Rahab's future was with the people of God: '... and she lives among the Israelites to this day' (6:25).

How would the Israelites cope with a former pagan prostitute living in their midst as one of them? Would they have rejoiced at the grace of God to a guilty sinner, or would they have kept her at arm's length, with a respectable tolerance but no real acceptance?

The churches in many lands today are made up of respectable middle-class men and women. The gospel we preach hardly touches society in general. But what if the gospel begins to bite into society and people with no church background are converted and begin to attend our churches? How would we cope with women from sexually immoral backgrounds that shock us? What about men whose lives have been dominated by drink and drugs and who, though now converted, are still fighting off the old temptations? Would they be welcomed as brothers and sisters in Christ? Would we invite them to our homes and befriend them, or merely tolerate them? And what about churches that for years have consisted only of people over the age of fifty? If we had an influx of young families with noisy children, could we cope? Or would we resent the presence of the youngsters and complain of their lack of reverence whilst we went on in reverent whispers to criticize the pastor's preaching and gossip about each other?

Thank God that he still saves the Rahabs of this world. But as Dale Ralph Davis points out, 'Now that can be offensive. We say we can't have that; the church is only for respectable, clean, middle-class folks. But that is like saying that hospitals are only for doctors, nurses, and x-ray machines instead of sick people... The church is not a club but a refuge for sinners who have been touched by the grace of God. Apparently, Rahab's past did not bother the writer of the first Gospel. Rather, Matthew seems to see in Rahab a trophy of divine grace. Astounding, isn't it, that the shady lady of Jericho should be the ancestress of Jesus the Messiah (Matthew 1:5)?'[5]

6.
Learning to trust God

Joshua 3

The Israelites were now in exactly the same position they had been in forty years previously. They were on the edge of the promised land and only the River Jordan separated them from their inheritance. Forty years ago they had listened to the fearful advice of the ten spies who had convinced them that it would be impossible to conquer the Canaanites (Num. 13). Joshua and Caleb had urged them to enter the land because 'The LORD is with us. Do not be afraid of them' (Num. 14:9). But fear had triumphed over faith, and the result was forty years in the wilderness. There is no doubt that the wilderness experience was divine judgement upon a redeemed people because of their unbelief.

The inheritance was still to come to God's people but not to that generation. All over the age of twenty years, except Caleb and Joshua, died in the desert. Their unbelief did not invalidate the gift, but it did delay it. It may well be true that today we are losing much of what God wants to give us because of our sin, unbelief and pride. There is so much in both Scripture and church history that we know nothing of, and we continue in a wilderness of dry, arid evangelicalism. Our doctrines are biblical but our experience of the blessings of God is negligible.

In the 1859 revival in Wales great things were happening under the preaching of David Morgan. One service in particular, at Devil's Bridge near Aberystwyth, was memorable. An old minister wrote of that service:

> The evening service was terrible. So near was the Revivalist to his God, that his face shone like that of an angel, so that none could gaze steadfastly at him. Many of the hearers swooned.
>
> On the way home I dared not break the silence for miles. Towards midnight I ventured to say, 'Didn't we have blessed meetings, Mr Morgan?'
>
> 'Yes', he replied; and after a pause, added, 'The Lord would give us great things if he could only trust us.'
>
> 'What do you mean?' I asked.
>
> 'If he could trust us not to steal the glory for ourselves.' Then the midnight air rang with his cry, at the top of his voice, 'Not unto us, O Lord, not unto us, but unto thy name give glory.' [1]

Is there anything more tragic in all the world than for God's people to miss out on so much blessing because God cannot trust us with his gifts, or refuses to pass on the promise because of our unbelief?

A test of faith

The spies Joshua sent out came back with a different message from that of their predecessors of forty years previously: 'The LORD has surely given the whole land into our hands; all the people are melting in fear because of us' (Josh. 2:24). This time there was no hesitation and the people made ready to cross the Jordan. Even though they were eager to proceed this was still a test of faith. Whatever the River Jordan is like today, in Joshua's time it clearly was a major obstacle and also it was in flood (3:15). Their willingness to go forward was because they had learnt the lesson of past failure. It is possible to learn a lesson too late, as the Israelites of Moses' day had discovered (see Num. 14:39-45).

This present generation, through spending forty years in the wilderness under God's judgement, had learnt to trust God for the basic necessities of food and clothing. Six days a week they saw a demonstration of the goodness of God in providing manna. And at the end of forty years Moses could make the remarkable claim of Deuteronomy 29:5: 'During the forty years that I led you through the desert, your clothes did not wear out, nor did the sandals on your feet.'

Faith is not a step in the dark, but a reasonable trust in a God who, time and time again, has proved his love for us and demonstrated his faithfulness. So here was Israel, on the edge of the Jordan, and the Lord was going to call upon them to trust him as never before. Here was a real testing of faith, but a testing of faith is also an opportunity to prove and strengthen faith. We ought not to look upon painful circumstances and difficult situations only as trials of faith to be endured, but rather regard them as golden opportunities to prove afresh the sufficiency of the Lord who never fails and never forsakes us. This is obviously easier said than done, but would not such an attitude totally change our lives? It would transform the dark times and keep us from mourning and depression. Is not our God worthy of such confidence and trust?

So God brought them to the Jordan and left them there for three days looking at the river in flood. There were no bridges; they had no boats and no idea of how to cross. Why did God do this? Was it not to teach them yet again that he was their only hope? A. W. Pink says, 'And is not that, very often, the chief design of God's providential dealings with us? To bring us to the end of our own resources, to make us conscious of our own insufficiency, by bringing us into a situation from which we cannot extricate ourselves, confronting us with some obstacle which to human wit and might is insurmountable? By nature we are proud and self-reliant, ignorant of the fact that the arm of flesh is frail, and even when faced with difficulties, we seek to resolve them by our own wisdom, or get out of a tight corner by our own efforts. But the Lord graciously resolved to humble us ... such dull scholars are we that, the lesson must be taught us again and yet again before we actually put it into practice.'[2]

The problems that confront us today as individual Christians and as churches are as frightening as Jordan must have been to Israel. We are never to minimize them, but neither are we to be daunted by them. We have a God greater than all the obstacles. He who opened the Jordan for Israel will deal with our difficulties in an equally emphatic way, but we must learn to trust and obey him.

The ark

The opening of the Jordan was not a freak of nature to be explained by a series of exceptional but natural events, any more than the opening of the Red Sea was. This was a miracle of God's grace and the people needed to know it. The ark of the covenant reminded them that God was at work. They were to follow the ark because, 'Then you will know which way to go, since you have never been this way before' (3:4).

The ark was a wooden box, four foot (120 cm.) by two foot six (76 cm.) by two foot six (76 cm), covered with gold. It was made under God's direction to hold the two stone tablets on which the Ten Commandments were written, a pot of manna and Aaron's staff that budded (Heb. 9:4). It was Israel's most holy object and symbolized the presence of God. When they followed the ark they were reminded of God's law, of his daily provision for them and of his setting men aside to lead and minister to them (Num. 17:1-11). More than that, the lid of the ark was made of solid gold and called the 'mercy-seat' (AV) or 'atonement cover' (NIV). Here the atoning blood of the sacrifice was sprinkled and the people were reminded, not only of their sin, but also of the mercy and love of God in dealing with that sin. The ark is called 'the ark of the covenant' to remind them of the special relationship they had with God. Everything about the ark testified to the goodness of God to his people.

The words of God

The Lord was going to exalt Joshua in the eyes of the people, but not so that they would delight in the man and praise him for their victories. The purpose was to show that God was with Joshua as he had been with Moses. The men are nothing apart from the Lord. So Joshua immediately reminds them that it is the Lord they are to obey: 'Come here and listen to the words of the LORD your God' (3:9). When a leadership is truly chosen and appointed by God it will be one that focuses the eyes of the people on the Lord, and not on the man.

It is one of the greatest privileges offered to the Christian that we can come and hear the words of the Lord. We should never minimize the value of this, never neglect it and never take it for granted. The word of God for them that day was one of reassurance (3:10-13). No matter how strong a man's faith may be, he will always need reassurance. The problems facing the Israelites were immense. They did not expect the tribes in Canaan to lie down and let them walk in. And how could they cope with battle after battle? Then there was the

immediate problem of Jordan in flood. In such situations —
and we all have to face them — it is not surprising if the devil
sows seeds of uncertainty in our minds. This will be particularly in times when God's word to us is, to put it mildly, strange
indeed: 'Tell the priests, who carry the ark of the covenant:
"When you reach the edge of the Jordan's waters, go and stand
in the river."'

What would you have done? There must have been something more practical to do than to get wet feet! And why after
forty years did God bring them to the Jordan at the exact time
when the river was in flood? His timing seemed to be all wrong.
If he had brought them there six months earlier the crossing
would have been much easier.

Such is the wisdom and logic of man. In times of extreme
stress it may appear that God's way is not very practical, and
we may be tempted to amend it or modernize it. We may come
to the conclusion that God's way will not work and we had
better try something else. When we are tempted to think like
that, remember Paul's words to the Corinthians: 'For since in
the wisdom of God the world through its wisdom did not know
him, God was pleased through the foolishness of what was
preached to save those who believe... For the foolishness of
God is wiser than man's wisdom, and the weakness of God is
stronger than man's strength... But God chose the foolish
things of the world to shame the wise; God chose the weak
things of the world to shame the strong ... so that no one may
boast before him' (1 Cor. 1:21,25, 27,29).

God's way, as revealed in Scripture, must be the way the
believer is to conduct all the affairs of his or her life. This,
then, is applicable to how we evangelize. Many seemingly
sound reasons can be given for arguing that in these days the
preaching of the gospel will not change anything in a godless
and materialistic world. We can be tempted to try something
else and forsake God's way. It is at times like this that we need

to hold our nerve, to keep our eyes on God and believe that his ways are always best. The lesson from Joshua at the Jordan is to do what you are told. But we must distinguish between the words of God and the traditions of men. The Pharisees made the basic mistake of giving an authority to tradition that only belongs to Scripture. Traditions are methods that we highly regard because they worked at a particular time in the past, but they may not work now. The teachings of Scripture always work, are always relevant, are always up to date — from these we dare not move an inch.

7.
Remembering what God has done

Joshua 4

In Joshua 3 God demonstrated in a miraculous way his love and care for his people by opening the barrier of the River Jordan. He could do this because, said Joshua, he is the living God (3:10) and the Lord of all the earth (3:13). For such a God to close off the Jordan is less trouble than for us to turn off a tap. But when God performs miracles he does not just do so as a means to an end. In these remarkable acts he is teaching necessary truths for our spiritual well-being. God could have held back the water without any fuss or bother, but he chose instead this way of having the priests stand in the river carrying the ark. The whole nation saw this and knew this was God's doing. It was not merely a matter of miracles, but of lessons to be learnt and truths to be applied concerning the goodness of God.

Two monuments

The lesson of the crossing of the Jordan was so important that God commanded Joshua to set up monuments, each made up of twelve stones taken from the middle of the river. One was to be set up in Gilgal, their first place to camp in the promised land. It seems also from Joshua 4:9 that another column of twelve stones was set up in the middle of the river. The NIV is rather confusing in verse 9. It seems to imply that this is just another reference to the twelve stones of Gilgal, but the alternative translation in the footnote says, 'Joshua also set up twelve stones in the middle of Jordan.' This is also the translation found in the New King James Version and the New American Standard Bible.

So there were two monuments, one at Gilgal as a memorial of their first encampment in Canaan, and the other in the bed of the river to mark the spot where they crossed.

Gilgal

The setting up of the twelve stones at Gilgal was not an empty gesture. It was done in response to a particular command of God and the reason was that 'These stones are to be a memorial to the people of Israel for ever' (4:7). We are all too prone to forget what the Lord does for us and such forgetfulness can be an enemy of faith. To forget means we lose a sense of gratitude and also a sense of expectancy. In the battles for Canaan the Israelites were going to need the Lord's intervention over and over again, and past blessings feed the expectancy for God to do again for his people his unique works. Warren Wiersbe reminds us that 'There is nothing wrong with memorials, provided they don't become religious idols that turn our hearts from God, and provided they don't so link us to the past that we fail to serve God in the present. Glorifying the past is a good way to petrify the present and rob the church of power. The next generations need reminders of what God has done in history, but these reminders must also strengthen their faith and draw them closer to the Lord.'[1]

The wonderful works of God are worth treasuring in our memories and God demands that we take the trouble to do so.

There were many things on Joshua's mind as he organized the nation's crossing of the Jordan. There were many responsibilities on his shoulders, but he was not to forget to promote the glory of his God. This is crucial for the spiritual well-being of future generations. There will be times of spiritual barrenness when blessings are few and far between. In many lands at the end of the twentieth century the church is experiencing such times. Empty churches and few conversions can be depressing, so we need to remind ourselves of what our God can do. Therefore, next to reading the Bible there is nothing more important than reading Christian biographies and church history. Christians who do not read these deprive themselves of great encouragement. Faith is nurtured by remembering what God has done. The apostle Peter reminds his readers of what God did for Noah and Lot to show them that 'The Lord knows how to rescue godly men from trials' (2 Peter 2:9). The Scriptures and church history are our twelve stones. We look back to the events recorded there and take comfort for present and future battles.

God deemed it necessary for a memorial to be erected at Gilgal because his people are so prone to forget his blessing. In Psalm 78:11 God accuses Israel of forgetting what he had done for them. The consequence of this was that they sinned against him by doubting his willingness and ability to supply their needs (Ps. 78:17-20). Jesus had to rebuke the apostles for failure to remember what he had done (Matt. 16:9). Such a failure led to confusion and a lack of understanding of his teaching. Is this not why Jesus commanded us to break bread and drink the wine 'in remembrance of me'? As if we could ever forget the cross! But God knows we could even forget that; hence the words of Jesus and the need of the memorial of the Lord's Supper.

We have just referred to Psalm 78 and it is significant to note in the opening eight verses how God is concerned with teaching children of his great deeds. Joshua puts the same emphasis to the people of his day: 'In the future when your children ask you, "What do these stones mean?" tell them that the flow of the Jordan was cut off before the ark of the covenant of the LORD.' The children's questions are to be answered by the parents, not by Joshua or the elders. The minds of our youngsters need to be provoked to ask questions, and these questions are to be dealt with by parents. Thank God for pastors, Sunday school teachers and youth leaders, but primarily the responsibility for teaching the children of Christians about God rests with the parents, particularly the father (4:6,21). To provoke such questions we should bring our children regularly to the services and ordinances of the church. If they do not see and hear such things, how can they ask, 'What do these mean?'

Unity

The twelve stones also serve to remind us of the unity of God's people. They spoke of the twelve tribes that made up the one nation. It was true that two and a half tribes had their inheritance on the east bank of the Jordan, but still they were one people and the twelve stones reminded them of this. There were many things in the history of Israel that would divide the people, but God always saw them as a unity and constantly reminded them of this. For instance, centuries later, the nation was divided into two kingdoms — Israel (ten tribes) and Judah (two tribes) — but in 1 Kings 18, when Elijah on Carmel rebuilt the altar, he did it with twelve stones: 'Elijah took twelve stones, one for each of the tribes descended from Jacob, to whom the word of the LORD had come, saying, "Your name shall be Israel." '

Today there are many things that divide God's people. Some are trivial and some are serious. We should never minimize the importance of doctrinal differences but even these are not to be allowed to break the unity of those whom Christ has saved with his blood. The doctrinal rift between John Wesley and George Whitefield was deep and some of Whitefield's followers began to doubt whether Wesley was truly converted. Arnold Dallimore tells us, 'Thus one of them once asked Whitefield if he expected to see Wesley in heaven, to which he replied: "I fear not, for he will be so near the eternal throne and we at such a distance we shall hardly get a sight of him." '[2]

More of that generous spirit of Whitefield is needed today to remind ourselves that whatever bank of the Jordan we make our doctrinal home, we are still one people.

8.
We belong to God

Joshua 5:1-12

After forty years in the wilderness the Israelites were probably eager to get on with fighting for the promised land, particularly so when they heard that the kings in the land had lost all stomach for battle. This was the obvious time to strike and they probably felt confident, but God kept them waiting. There were still preparatory things to be done among them. In chapter 5 we see what these were — the reintroduction of circumcision, the celebration of the Passover and Joshua's amazing meeting with the Lord.

It did not really matter whether the Canaanites were afraid or whether they were brimming with confidence. They were not the problem. The omnipotent God had already decreed that they would not win but, as ever, Israel was the problem. God's own people always caused him more problems than the unbelieving masses. This is very clearly revealed in the battles in the book of Judges, particularly Gideon's battle with the Midianites. God would give them the victory, but he was concerned that Israel should not boast that she had won the victory by her own strength (Judg. 7:2). God reduced Gideon's army to 300 soldiers so there could be no doubt where the victory came from. Perhaps if the Lord could trust us more we would see more victories in our lives! Perhaps if we trusted him more instead of relying upon our own strength we would

see the church making greater progress in overcoming the
enemies of darkness in this world!

Circumcision was the sign of the covenant, the sign that
they were God's people, but for forty years it had not been
observed. Before the fighting began this had to be rectified.

At that time

'At that time' (5:2) is a significant phrase. It refers to something special having happened. This was the time when God
brought them from the judgement of the wilderness, the time
when they first set foot in the promised land; and the time
before the task began of taking possession of their inheritance. At that time, following the activity and excitement of
crossing the river, and before the involvement in the battle for
Jericho, God brought everything to a halt. All the men under
the age of forty were to be circumcised and this, of course,
meant that they had to remain 'where they were in camp until
they were healed' (5:8).

There are some things much more important than activity
and by far the most important is to be aware that we are God's
people. Circumcision was the sign of the covenant. It was a
mark in their bodies that they belonged to God. The Lord had
always put a great importance upon this sign. This is seen in
Exodus 4 when the Lord was about to kill Moses because he
had failed to circumcise his son.

Why Israel had neglected circumcision for forty years is
not clear. There is no account of Moses rebuking them because of this, so it was probably not sinful neglect. Some have
suggested that the Lord himself withdrew the sign after they
refused to enter the promised land. The unbelief of Israel
reached its depth at this point and particularly when they wanted
to return to Egypt. It was then that God declared they would
never receive the promised inheritance: 'Not one of you will

enter the land I swore with uplifted hand to make your home, except Caleb son of Jephunneh and Joshua son of Nun. As for your children that you said would be taken as plunder, I will bring them in to enjoy the land you have rejected. But you — your bodies will fall in this desert. Your children will be shepherds here for forty years, suffering for your unfaithfulness, until the last of your bodies lies in the desert. For forty years — one year for each of the forty days you explored the land — you will suffer for your sins and know what it is like to have me against you' (Num. 14:30-34).

God being against them was a terrible experience and it could be that this involved their children being denied the sign of the covenant. Dale Ralph Davis says, 'In light of Genesis 17:14 one can say that this lack of circumcision was a sign that Israel was "cut off" (because of their unbelief?). They were God's people and yet they were not; they remained objects of God's care and yet possessed no sign to show they were his.'[1] But God had not finished with the children and they were assured that they would enjoy the land after the forty years in the wilderness saw the death of all the older ones except Joshua and Caleb.

The time had now come for that promise to be fulfilled and this involved the need for them all to be circumcised. The word 'again' in verse 2 does not mean circumcise them a second time, but to restore again the long absent sign. The 'reproach of Egypt' was now a thing of the past and a new start was to be theirs, with the Lord not now against them, but very much for them.

Spiritual circumcision

The problem with signs, even those instigated by God, is that we can come to trust in them and not in the Lord. Wiersbe says, 'But over the years, the Jews came to trust in the external mark of the covenant and not in the God of the covenant who wanted to make them a holy people. They thought that as long as they were God's covenant people, they could live just as they pleased; Moses warned them about this sin (Deut. 30:6), and so did the prophets (Jer. 4:4). When John the Baptist called them to repent, the Jewish spiritual leaders said, "We have Abraham as our father." They were not unlike some people today who feel sure they are saved and going to heaven because they are baptized, confirmed, and participate regularly in communion. As good as these religious rites can be, they must never become substitutes for faith in Jesus Christ.'[2]

The Lord had warned Israel about this when he called upon them to 'Circumcise your hearts, therefore, and do not be stiff-necked any longer' (Deut. 10:16). In the New Testament Paul again issues the same warning in Romans 2:25-29: 'Circumcision has value if you observe the law, but if you break the law, you have become as though you had not been circumcised. If those who are not circumcised keep the law's requirements, will they not be regarded as though they were circumcised? The one who is not circumcised physically and yet obeys the law will condemn you who, even though you have the written code and circumcision, are a lawbreaker. A man is not a Jew if he is only one outwardly, nor is circumcision merely outward and physical. No, a man is a Jew if he is one inwardly; and circumcision is circumcision of the heart, by the Spirit, not by the written code. Such a man's praise is not from men, but from God.'

Commenting on these verses Dr Lloyd-Jones wrote, 'What makes a man a Jew, says the apostle Paul, is not primarily that he belongs to a particular nation, it is not a matter of national attachment, or some external position. What then? Ah, he says, it is an inward state. It is exactly the same with circumcision. That which is really circumcision is not something external, in the flesh, as the Jews thought; it is something of the heart and of the spirit, of the inner man. It is not something merely in the letter but is an inward process — that is, an external sign of some inward grace, of some inward operation. God gave it externally, merely to help them, but the real thing is within.'[3]

All Christians are circumcised spiritually in Christ (Col. 2:10-11). This circumcision is not done by the hands of men. This distinguishes it from the physical circumcision of the Old Testament and shows it is not something we can do ourselves. The greatest sign that we belong to God is that we are in Christ, that he has done something to us that has changed our lives. We no longer live for self, but for Christ. We are new creations, living in a way that honours and pleases our Lord. Signs are no substitute for reality and whatever else may or may not be true of a Christian, this reality of a living faith needs to shine out. It is no use having some outward mark of being a Christian, whether it is baptism or church membership, if our hearts are in rebellion against the word and law of God.

The Passover

Israel had been in Egypt for a long time and, over the years, something of Egypt had got into them. They had become acclimatized to the sin and idolatry of Egypt. Even when God had set them free, there was always the temptation to look back longingly. This is amazing considering they were slaves in that land, but sin is a greater bondage than anything Pharaoh could impose. Sin blinds and distorts. It reduces everything to the same level of dissatisfaction with, and rebellion against, God. Just before he led them from Egypt the Lord said that he would make a distinction between Egypt and Israel (Exod. 11:7). That distinction was the blood of the Passover lamb. When judgement came to the land it was the blood that saved the Israelites from death. This was an event never to be forgotten and led directly to their leaving the life of slavery. They had celebrated the Passover again on the first anniversary of the event in the wilderness, but not since. When God forbade circumcision he also in effect forbade the Passover because he had commanded that no uncircumcised man should eat the Passover meal. But now there was a new beginning and the Passover was celebrated for the first time in nearly forty years.

The Passover was meant by God to be a lasting ordinance for his people (Exod. 12:14), but their sin had robbed them of this blessing. However, the grace of God that provided the original Passover is able to deal with sin, and grace comes again to the people as they not only remember the event of forty years ago but also celebrate the new blessing of actually being in the promised land.

With the entry to Canaan came the end of the temporary blessing of the manna. Now they could eat the produce of the land itself. This was no less a gift from God than the manna had been, but whereas one was miraculous and temporary, the other was natural and permanent. Davis says, 'Most of God's gifts to his people are not dazzling and gaudy but wrapped in simple brown paper. Quiet provisions of safety on the highway, health of children, picking up a pay-cheque, supper with the family — all in an ordinary day's work for our God.'[4]

The manna was a supernatural blessing of God to his people in a time of judgement, but it was only a substitute for the real blessing, which was a land flowing with milk and honey.

9.
The Lord is our Captain

Joshua 5:13-15

The wilderness time for Israel had come to an end, but what about us? Western Europe at the end of the twentieth century knows little if anything of the rich spiritual blessings our forefathers knew. If we know something of church history we can appreciate the wonders of God which earlier generations have experienced — the revivals, the great preachers, the packed churches, the impact the Bible made upon the laws of the nation. But that is history and sadly it is not our experience today. It seems as if we are in a spiritual wilderness. Like Israel in the desert we still know something of God's mercies because we are his people. We see a few souls saved, and now and again the prayer meeting seems to come alive with a sense of the presence of God — but not often. We are not to despise the day of small things but neither are we to be satisfied with it as if that is all we can expect. Who wants manna when there is the possibility of the fruit of the land?

Do we want to stay in the wilderness? Are we content with substitute blessings? The answer has to be 'No', but how do we change the situation? We see the answer in the book of Joshua. God was dealing with his people and they were learning anew who they were. Circumcision spoke of the special covenant relationship they had with God. Passover reminded them of the redemptive power and grace of God working for

them. If the grace of God that has placed us in a special relationship with the Lord is becoming more real to us, then we
can be hopeful that God is also dealing with us and preparing
us for blessing. But let us not forget that the blessings God
had in store for Joshua and his people were not the blessings
of ease and comfort but of battle. The promised land was the
gift of God's free grace but they had to fight for every inch of
it. That may not appeal to some, but we need to remember
that the battles were won, and it is better to be in a battle with
the Lord's help than in the spiritual wilderness under God's
judgement.

God in human form

The restoration of circumcision and the Passover were the
last preparations for Israel as a prelude to the fulfilment of the
age-old promise of a promised land. There was one last thing
that Joshua himself needed if he was to lead the people with
confidence and faithfulness. The encounter with the man near
Jericho (5:13-15) is both thrilling and crucial for anyone who
is called to work for God. Wiersbe says, 'This paragraph
records one of the pre-incarnation appearances of the Lord
Jesus Christ recorded in the Old Testament. To Abraham the
pilgrim, the Lord came as a traveller to share in a friendly meal
(Gen. 18:1-8). To Jacob the schemer, he came as a wrestler to
bring him to the place of submission (32:24-32). The three
Hebrew men met him as their companion in the furnace of fire
(Dan. 3:25), and Joshua met him as the Captain of the Lord's
armies. Our Lord always comes to us when we need him and
in the way we need him. It must have been a great encouragement to Joshua to realize that he was not alone. There is a
loneliness to leadership that can be disturbing and even depressing as you realize how much your decisions affect the
lives of others.'[1]

It seems that Joshua was on his own near Jericho. He knew that there was no bypassing this city. It had to be conquered if they were to realize their dream of possessing the land. Joshua was confident that the Lord would be with him, but he knew there could be no short cuts to victory. Jericho had to be dealt with — but how? Perhaps he came to look at the city to assess tactics. God had not yet told him how to conduct the battle, so he was acting responsibly as the leader in assessing the situation. It is not spiritual to sit back idly and say, 'The Lord will provide.' We are responsible beings and have to use any ability God has given us to make progress in the spiritual battles.

It was while Joshua was faithfully following his duty that he had this remarkable experience. This was not a vision but a theophany. In the Old Testament there are several appearances of God in human form to men. These are called theophanies. The purpose is usually twofold: to encourage his people at a particular time, and to foreshadow the most glorious appearance of all, when Christ not only took human form but also human nature. And this was not for a brief moment but for all eternity. The coming of Christ to this world was not technically a theophany but an incarnation, not just a temporary form but God becoming man; God not just appearing to man but identifying himself with us by adding human nature to his divine nature; God not coming to us with a temporary encouragement but with an eternal salvation.

The meeting

Joshua saw a man with a drawn sword, obviously ready for battle. This may have seemed provocative to Joshua, so he asked what was for him the obvious question: 'Are you for us or for our enemies?' To him there was no other position in the circumstance of the coming battle. The unknown man needed to make his position clear. If the stranger had been a mere man then Joshua would have been right, but the answer he received makes clear that this was no mere man. The man had not come to offer his sword to one side or the other, but to take charge — he was the commander of the army of the Lord. He was the Christ and he had come, not to offer his help to Joshua, but to tell Joshua what to do.

Ignorance as to whom he was dealing with led Joshua to put Christ into a convenient category — them or us. When the people of Jesus' time were asked who they thought he was, they did the same thing. They said he was Jeremiah or Elijah — in fact all the categories they put him in suggested a high and respectful opinion of Jesus, but it was not high enough. He is not man — not even the greatest of men; he is the Christ of God and therefore in a category all his own.

When Joshua realized who it was he was dealing with there was for him only one response, and he fell to the ground in reverence. That this was appropriate is confirmed by the Lord's response: 'Take off your sandals, for the place where you are standing is holy.' Joshua had the Book of the Law and he would have read there of Moses at the burning bush and the same words being used (Exod. 3:5). Without a moment's hesitation he did as he was told.

Christ today

The New Testament makes it plain that Christ still draws near to his people. It may not be in a theophany — we no longer need that when we have an incarnation — but he does make his presence felt and we all need such an encounter with Jesus. There is too much in modern Christianity that is trite, flippant and unholy. It is not just the charismatics who are guilty of this; what about those of us who believe the reformed doctrines? Are we any better? Is Jesus real to us? It is noticeable in many reformed churches how easy it is to switch from deeply spiritual things in the sermon to completely material matters in our conversations afterwards. It is as if Jesus ceases to have any relevance after the benediction. Even though we believe the right doctrines, Jesus himself is a stranger to us. We desperately need today to know the living presence of Christ in our midst.

Joshua's encounter outside Jericho gives us pointers on how to experience this. The meeting with the commander of the Lord's army was the culmination of other things. First of all, there had been the circumcision, or an awareness that they were God's people. Then came the Passover, or an awareness of God's grace and power in redemption. We need to recapture once more the realization of these great truths. If you are a Christian, you are:

chosen of God;
loved with an everlasting love;
the apple of God's eye;
precious to God;
redeemed by the blood of Christ;
indwelt by the Holy Spirit;
saved from hell and guaranteed a place in heaven.

These great truths need to be real to us. They are more than doctrines. They ought to be the experience that we live by every day. The awareness of the presence of Jesus is not the result of an emotional experience, but the product of biblical truths being firmly fixed in our minds and felt in our hearts.

When Jesus draws near he always comes to take charge. His instructions, as we shall see in the next chapter, may not always be what we would anticipate, but they always lead to victory. His nearness will make us aware of the holiness of our God and then reverence, not flippancy, becomes inevitable.

Spurgeon urges us, 'If you desire to see Christ you must grow to be like him, and labour to serve him with heart, and soul, and strength. Christ comes not in the visions of the night to those who toss upon the bed of indolence, but he reveals himself in the night watches to those who learn to watch and war. Bring yourselves, by the power of the Spirit, into union with Christ's desires, and motives, and plans of action, and you are likely to see him. I would that all of you were Joshuas; but if not, if but some shall perceive him, we shall still receive a blessing.'[2]

10.
God will fight the battle

Joshua 6

Jericho seems to have been Canaan's strongest city, so Israel's first task in the promised land was an immense one. But Jericho had to be overcome if God's gift of a country to live in was to be opened up. The King of Jericho had no confidence to face Joshua's army openly because he knew God's power was working for the Israelites. In spite of this he seemed to be fairly confident in the strength and security of the city's walls. This was his only hope and so 'Jericho was tightly shut up because of the Israelites' (6:1).

Jericho is thought to be the oldest-known continually occupied human settlement and its walls represent the first technology that can be ascribed to purely military purposes. It was seeing cities like this that had led the ten spies forty years earlier to conclude that Israel had no hope of conquering Canaan: 'The cities are large, with walls up to the sky' (Deut. 1:28). As Joshua viewed this immense obstacle he must have wondered how he could breach these walls. At that point the Lord said to him, 'I have delivered Jericho into your hands' (6:2). Not 'I will', but 'I have' — it is as good as done, it is an accomplished fact.

The old Negro spiritual says, 'Joshua fought the battle of Jericho,' but in fact there was no actual battle. God gave them the city without Israel having to strike a single blow. Having said that, we must admit that the Lord's method for bringing down the walls was a great test of the people's faith.

The Canaanites

The Canaanites were afraid of God's people and refused to come out openly and fight them. At this point the Israelites must have thought the conquest of the promised land was going to be easy. It is the exact opposite today; now the world has no fear of the Christian church. The gates to the world's pleasures are not shut tight to keep us out, but open wide, and Christians seem eager to flock through to enjoy all that God forbids. The world has nothing to fear from the church because we are too much like it.

Cwmbran (pronounced Cumbran) is the only 'new town' in Wales, a town that was built in the 1950s to house workers from the huge new steelworks nearby. In the early years of its development the authorities decided to commission a statue to stand in the shopping centre depicting a family in the new town, comprised of father, mother and child. One day the statue appeared in its designated spot, all boarded up, awaiting the official unveiling ceremony. People were naturally curious to see what it looked like. Then the great day came and the statue was unveiled. People gasped with amazement at what they saw. The following comments were actually heard:

'What is it?'

'It looks like three drunken worms.'

'It looked better with the boards up.'

The statue caused a great commotion. TV crews came to see and record. The newspapers interviewed people for their opinion on the statue, and everyone had a view to express. What caused the stir was that the statue was in the style of modern art, and very few people liked or understood it. If it had been a conventional statue no one would have given it a second look. It was the difference that caused people to sit up and take notice.

The Christians in the Acts of the Apostles caused a stir everywhere they went because they were different. Their lives, actions, ambitions and beliefs were different, and people took note of them. Today we try desperately to make our faith acceptable to people by making our Christianity no different from their lifestyle. We try to show them that really we are exactly like them. The result is that the church has no effect upon the world. The world ignores us. Why should it bother if we are no different?

The Israelites throughout their history were exactly the same. Psalm 78 recounts their continuous rebellion against God right up to the time they entered the promised land:

> Thus he brought them to the border of his holy land,
>   to the hill country his right hand had taken.
> He drove out nations before them
>   and allotted their lands to them as an inheritance;
>   he settled the tribes of Israel in their homes.
> But they put God to the test
>   and rebelled against the Most High;
>   they did not keep his statutes.
> Like their fathers they were disloyal and faithless,
>   as unreliable as a faulty bow
>
> (Ps. 78:54-57).

What they forgot, and what we forget too, is that we are not to 'love the world or anything in the world. If anyone loves the world, the love of the Father is not in him' (1 John 2:15). The Canaanites represented everything that God hated. In Genesis 15:16 God told Abraham that it would be the fourth generation of his descendants who would conquer Canaan. The reason given for this delay was: 'For the sin of the Amorites has not yet reached its full measure.' Leupold says, 'All the inhabitants of Canaan are referred to by the term "Amorites," the most important family of the Canaanites... These aboriginal inhabitants of Canaan had heaped up a measure of guilt by this time. The measure was not yet complete, that is, they were nearing the point when divine tolerance could bear with them no longer, but they had not yet arrived at this point.'[1]

What was their sin that reached its full measure in Joshua's time? In Leviticus 18:1-23 God lists what he regards as gross sexual perversions, then he immediately says, 'Do not defile yourselves in any of these ways, because this is how the nations I am going to drive out before you became defiled. Even the land was defiled; so I punished it for its sin, and the land vomited out its inhabitants.' Then in Deuteronomy 18 we see that the Canaanites practised magic and sorcery including human sacrifices, and once more we are told how God regards such things: 'Anyone who does these things is detestable to the LORD, and because of these detestable practices the LORD your God will drive out those nations before you' (Deut. 18:12).

When God drove these people from the land it was not an act of barbaric injustice. Davis writes, 'The conquest is not a bunch of land-hungry marauders wiping out, at the behest of their vicious God, hundreds of innocent, God-fearing folks. In the biblical view, the God of the Bible uses none-too-righteous Israel as the instrument of his just punishment on a people who had persistently revelled in their iniquity.'[2]

The conquest of Canaan was a divine judgement and Israel was God's tool in this.

A strange method

If there is one recurring certainty in Scripture it is that God's ways are not our ways. In all his dealings with us, because of our pride and arrogance, God has to make sure that we do not rob him of his glory. When he reduced Gideon's army to three hundred he did so 'in order that Israel may not boast against me that her own strength has saved her' (Judg. 7:2).

It was exactly the same at Jericho. There was no precedent for what the Lord told Joshua to do. There were to be no battering rams, no siege towers, no normal military procedures. They were to 'March around the city once with all the armed men. Do this for six days. Make seven priests carry trumpets of rams' horns in front of the ark. On the seventh day, march around the city seven times, with the priests blowing the trumpets. When you hear them sound a long blast on the trumpets, make all the people give a loud shout; then the wall of the city will collapse and the people will go up, every man straight in' (6:4-5).

Joshua had had that remarkable meeting with the pre-incarnate Christ so it was not surprising that he voiced no doubts as to the wisdom of this strange method. What is amazing is that Scripture records not one complaint or groan from the rest of the people. Their response was one of faith: 'By faith the walls of Jericho fell, after the people had marched around them for seven days' (Heb. 11:30). Faith is not an irresponsible step into the unknown, but a reasonable obedience to the will and word of a sovereign, almighty God.

The tasks facing Christians at the end of the twentieth century are no less daunting than were the walls of Jericho to Joshua. It has always been the same. In the first century Paul, with all his intellect and gifts, facing the problems he had to deal with said, 'Who is equal to such a task?' (2 Cor. 2:16). Nothing Paul had by way of natural abilities could break the hold of sin in people's lives. That is why he told the Corinthian church that when he came to them he had no confidence in his own abilities but was totally dependent on a demonstration of the Spirit's power. Whether it is God working through Joshua at Jericho, or through Paul at Corinth, or through us today, the basic principle is always true: 'The weapons we fight with are not the weapons of the world. On the contrary, they have divine power to demolish strongholds' (2 Cor. 10:4).

One Sunday during the 1859 revival a country church in Wales had no recognized preacher in the pulpit. Great things were happening in the land and thousands were coming to faith in Christ, but on this Sunday no one was expecting much blessing. In the prayer meeting before the service one man prayed, 'Lord, you know that we have no great preacher here today.' He went on to describe some preachers as like a beautiful suit of clothes, but their preacher that day was just a tatty old sleeve.

To everyone's surprise, the preacher was mightily used by God and many were saved. It was recognized that though the preacher was only 'a tatty old sleeve', God's arm had filled the sleeve and great blessing flowed.

We need to see again today God's arm filling the 'tatty old sleeve'. When that happens our lack-lustre efforts are transformed and ordinary preachers become infused with power.

The man God used in a remarkable way in Wales during the 1859 revival was a Presbyterian minister named David Morgan. He had exercised a very ordinary ministry for a number of years, but he said that one night he went to bed like a lamb and woke up like a lion. The power of the Holy Spirit had come upon him. Eifion Evans writes of David Morgan: 'Though he had sought the blessing for years, he was abashed when he realized that it was at hand, awaiting his acceptation. He retired to rest at his usual time on Tuesday evening, and slept for some hours. He awoke about 5 a.m., and was instantly conscious that some strange, mysterious change had come over him. He became aware with awe of a marvellous illumination of his faculties, especially of his memory. "I woke about 4 in the morning", said he himself, "remembering everything of a religious nature that I had ever learnt or heard." '[3]

With such divine power at work not only the walls of Jericho but also the sinful defences of London, New York and all the great modern cities would fall before our God.

Around the city

The weapons that brought down the walls of Jericho were not the usual instruments of war but the ark of the covenant and seven trumpets made of ram's horns. The people's contribution was the walk around the city in silence. It must have been an unnerving sight for the inhabitants of Jericho on the walls watching the solemn procession of silent figures. Strange though the command was, the Israelites followed it to the letter. Did the walls then fall down? No, the people returned to camp and bedded down for the night. Nothing had changed. The walls were as strong as ever. But something had happened: God had been honoured and glorified because nothing so honours God as our obedience. To judge events only by what appears to happen is always a great mistake in Christian work. So too is an impatient spirit that wants to speed up God's timetable. It is possible to get results without honouring and glorifying God. A battering ram, or even surrender negotiations, might have brought victory at Jericho sooner, but the only complete and ultimate victory came through obedience to God's way.

Verse 12 tells us that Joshua was up early the next day eager to get the people back into God's path of victory. This went on for six days. It was faith in the promise of God that kept them going. Scripture tells us not to grow weary in well doing. Faith is not some glamorous, easy way. It is hard graft and requires staying power and patient obedience. God could have brought the walls down after the first or any other day. The seven days of walking were not for the purpose of bringing the walls down, but to teach his people the simple but difficult lesson of complete obedience. Sometimes God tests our love by taking us through circumstances that seem strange — circumstances that well-nigh bring us to despair with a sense of hopelessness. In frustration we cry out, 'Why doesn't God do something?' But he is doing something — he is testing our faith. The path of faith is not easy and one of the most painful discoveries in the Christian life is that God has ordained disappointments for us as well as victories. These disappointments can have a crucial influence upon strengthening and deepening our experience of God. One of the Puritans said, 'Grace grows better in winter.'

On the seventh day the people were up at daybreak because on this day they had to go around the city not once, but seven times. It was not getting any easier, but harder! God was demanding more trust and faith now than on the first day. It was only after they had completely obeyed all God's instructions and had gone around seven times on the seventh day that Joshua told them, 'The LORD has given you the city.' Up to this point they had heard from Joshua the commands of God, but not this specific promise. They had not been obedient in order to gain the promise, but because obedience to God is right in and of itself, whether there is a reward or not.

If we follow Christ only because of what we can get out of it in terms of material blessings, we have a totally wrong understanding of God. Such an attitude betrays a heart that knows nothing of true faith. The promises of God are precious and to be treasured. They are to be looked for and expected, but our obsession should be to honour and glorify God by our obedience to his commands. This is the evidence of love for God, says Jesus: 'If you love me, you will obey what I command' (John 14:15).

11.
Sin has consequences

Joshua 7

Joshua 7 opens with a very ominous 'but', and introduces us to a whole new experience of Israel in the promised land. Blessing and victory are replaced with humiliation and defeat. Once again we see how crucial obedience is. The people had been warned very clearly before the walls of Jericho fell: 'But keep away from the devoted things, so that you will not bring about your own destruction by taking any of them. Otherwise you will make the camp of Israel liable to destruction and bring trouble on it' (6:18). The 'devoted' things were those mentioned in verse 19 — silver, gold, etc. In fact everything in the city was to be devoted to God. There were no spoils of war; everything had to be put into the treasury. The command was very clear and all the people faithfully obeyed, except one.

One man's sin

Achan's sin was the act of an individual, but the consequence for the nation was enormous. The language of 7:1 is frightening: 'The Israelites acted unfaithfully... So the LORD's anger burned against Israel.' Then again in verse 11 the Lord says, 'Israel has sinned.' God regarded them as a unit and so the sin of one is regarded as the sin of all. Our reaction may well be that this is unfair; if so we had better wake up to the fact that this is how God regards his people. The church 'is a unit, though it is made up of many parts; and though all its parts are many, they form one body' (1 Cor. 12:12). Because this is true, 'If one part suffers, every part suffers with it' (1 Cor. 12:26). Israel had been clearly warned that if any individual sinned by taking what belonged to God then the whole nation would be held accountable.

We need to realize that as Christians we cannot live for ourselves. Everything we do as believers affects other Christians and this is particularly true in the local church. Directly or indirectly, we all influence each other for good or evil. Therefore we have no right to say, 'I don't care what anyone else thinks. I will please myself.' We gave up the right to talk like that when we were converted. If it is true that even Christ did not please himself (Rom. 15:3), then we certainly are not free to do so. 'Please yourself. Do your own thing'— this is the language of the devil.

God tells us that we are members of the body of Christ. We are part of the church, part of a fellowship. This being so, we are commanded to love each other and to be concerned for each other's well-being. We are encouraged to be like Lydia, whose house was opened to God's people. We are pointed to Philemon, who was a refreshment to the saints. This is all so different from the 'please-yourself' attitude. If we as Christians live like this it is certain that, though we may please ourselves, we do not please the Lord.

Achan's sin was that:

He did not take the warning of God seriously (6:18-19).
He coveted that which was not his (7:21).
He thought he could hide his wrong (7:21).
He saw as plunder what belonged to God (7:21).

There is nothing particularly unusual about Achan's sin. It is common enough among us all but, whereas we can see the consequence of this man's action, can we see what our sin is doing to our church? What blessing are we personally responsible for holding back? We can be thankful that the Lord does not deal with us exactly as he did with Achan, and with Ananias and Sapphira in Acts 5, but he still deals with us. Worldliness, carnality, gossip and criticism are sins common enough in any church and perhaps this is why our churches are so powerless.

God's anger

After the easy victory at Jericho came the surprising defeat at the smaller city of Ai. Clearly Achan's sin was the main reason for this but a contributory factor was the overconfidence of the people generally. It is not difficult to see where this overconfidence came from. There is a certain logic about the assumption that they would not need as many men to defeat Ai as they did Jericho. But what they had not learnt is that everything depended upon the Lord. Even Joshua did not object to their reasoning and there was no word from God to prevent them from following their disastrous plan. The reason for this is that when God is angry with his people nothing will be right. If they had not been overconfident and had taken the whole army to Ai, the result would still have been the same. God's anger is a serious business for Christians and must never be taken lightly. Matthew Henry says, 'True Israelites tremble when God is angry.'[1]

Joshua bewildered

Thirty-six Israelites died at Ai and the 3,000 soldiers who attacked the city were routed. Poor Joshua was in confusion and bewilderment. How could this have happened? From a spiritual perspective with the almighty God on their side, they should not have lost. Even from a military perspective Ai should have been no problem. Yet the fact was, thirty-six men were dead and the whole nation was demoralized. Whilst Joshua knew nothing of Achan's sin, he must have been aware that the defeat was God's doing. There was no other reasonable explanation considering all that had preceded Ai — meeting with Christ, crossing Jordan and the manner of the victory at Jericho.

Joshua's prayer in verses 6-9 reveals several significant factors in his thinking. In the shock of the defeat he forgot the initial promise of God in chapter 1:3-9. This was the solid foundation on which everything else depended. But the pressure of the defeat clouded his thinking. His prayer seems to assume that the one defeat was a total defeat. Instead of inheriting the promised land, Israel would now be wiped out. Joshua sinks to using the same sort of language the unbelieving people had used on a previous occasion: 'Why did we leave Egypt? Why did we cross Jordan?'

Disappointment, sorrows and pressures cause the providence of God to be lost sight of. Are we not all guilty of this? Something goes wrong and in our pain and confusion we write everything off. It may be our faith, or our church, or our pastor. The problem is that we stop thinking and start reacting. We forget all that God has done for us, and the present disaster obliterates everything else. Our reaction is almost inevitably short-sighted; it lacks perspective and gratitude; it is unable rightly to assess a situation; it will seek simplistic solutions and will nearly always lead a Christian to blame God for the mess in which he finds himself.

Joshua was a remarkable man — otherwise God would never have chosen him to lead the people; but even the remarkable man is capable of a foolish reaction. Apart from the grace of God we are all like leaves in the wind, with no stability, no direction and no control. God's response to his servant in this state of confusion was to shock him into action — stop praying and start sorting out the problem.

Sin changes things

One of the most foolish of all human attitudes is to think that sin does not make any difference. From Adam and Eve onwards this seems to mark human thought and behaviour. What possible harm could come from Eve's picking one piece of fruit? And today sin is applauded as if it is just a harmless human entertainment. The difference sin makes is clearly seen in society with the breakdown of marriages, the drug problem and a whole medley of despair and unhappiness in the world.

Achan's sin was devastating for Israel. Thirty-six men were dead, but by far the worst consequence was the threat that God would no longer be with the people unless the sin was dealt with. Better military tactics or more sophisticated weapons would achieve nothing: 'You cannot stand against your enemies until you remove it' (7:13). Even prayer became superfluous until the sin was routed out. That was the seriousness of the situation facing Joshua, and it is always the same. Prayer is no substitute for repentance. God always deals with sin amongst his people by withdrawing his blessings. He never stops loving them, as we can see in Psalm 89:

> If his sons forsake my law
>   and do not follow my statues,
> if they violate my decrees
>   and fail to keep my commands,
> I will punish their sin with the rod,
>   their iniquity with flogging;

but I will not take my love from him,
   nor will I ever betray my faithfulness.
I will not violate my covenant
   or alter what my lips have uttered
                                        (Ps. 89:30-34).

Whilst there is no condemnation to those who are in Christ, this does not mean that the Lord will turn a blind eye to our sin. That sin will not take us to hell — the blood of Christ has dealt with that once and for all — but it will rob us of God's present blessings. And on occasions it can bring what Psalm 89 calls God dealing with our sin by applying the rod. For the people of Joshua's time that meant the defeat at Ai, with all its consequences. For the Corinthian church it meant that 'Many among you are weak and sick, and a number of you have fallen asleep' (1 Cor. 11:30). This does not mean that all sickness is a direct consequence of a particular sin, but it does mean that God will use defeat, humiliation, sickness, or anything else, to deal with our sin if we do not deal with it. One thing we can be sure of is that God always deals with sin.

Firstly, he exposes it in order that this will bring repentance from us. King David seemed to go on happily in his sin after the Bathsheba affair for a year or so until God sent the prophet to accuse him: 'You are the man.' This lead to the repentance of Psalm 51. When the sin that caused the defeat at Ai was first announced there was no individual's name attached to it. At that point Achan could have come forward and made confession, but he did not. God's way of revealing the guilty one by going through the nation by tribe, then by clan, then by family, was drawn out and gave Achan ample opportunity for confession, but he said nothing until he was forced to. There was no repentance and therefore no forgiveness.

This chapter is a very sad story. Davis said of it that 'You cannot treat cancer with vitamin pills; it requires radical surgery.'[2] But there is a ray of hope here too. Wiersbe says, 'The death of Achan and his family was certainly a dramatic warning to the nation not to take the Word of God lightly. The people and the animals were stoned, and their bodies burnt along with all that the family possessed. The troubler of Israel was completely removed from the scene, the people were sanctified, and now God could march with his people and give them victory. The name *Achor* means "trouble". The Valley of Achor is mentioned in Isaiah 65:10 and Hosea 2:15 as a place where the Jews will one day have a new beginning and no longer be associated with shame and defeat. The Valley of Achor will become for them "a door of hope" when they return to their land and share in the blessings of the messianic kingdom. How wonderful the Lord is to take Achor, a place of sorrow and defeat, and make it into a place of hope and joy.'[3]

12.
Recovering from discouragements

Joshua 8

Joshua 7 concludes, 'Then the LORD turned from his fierce anger...' When God shows us our sin he expects us to deal ruthlessly with it. If we do, then his anger is turned away and he begins again to deal in mercy and blessing with his people. The opening words of chapter 8 are meant to encourage a demoralized and humiliated people. They had certainly lost hope of taking possession of the promised land and now that Achan had been dealt with they needed to be assured that everything was back on track. At the end of the chapter they are brought back very pointedly to the law of God but before even that their hope needed to be renewed.

Encouragement

The people of Israel had been humiliated at Ai but, worse than that, they had felt the reality of God's anger. It is always a mark of a spiritual man that when he knows he has grieved God, he himself is grieved and dejected. This is because his relationship to God is the all-important thing in his life, far surpassing anything else. So even when sin is repented of he still needs to know again a sure sign of God's favour. There is nothing more important to the Christian than this. The depressed Peter after his denial of Christ desperately needed the assurance Jesus gave him after the resurrection on the shore of Galilee that there was still a ministry for him. The Lord's command that he was to feed Christ's sheep must have been like a new beginning for him.

God said to Joshua, 'Do not be afraid; do not be discouraged,' because he and all the people were very much afraid and discouraged. Joshua did not take God for granted. He had seen the awfulness of divine wrath dealing with sin and it would have been surprising if he had not felt as he did. But where there is godly sorrow and true repentance there will always be forgiveness. As Christians we need to remember this because the devil would have us lie forever under a burden of hopelessness. The words of 1 John 1:9 are written to believers, not unbelievers: 'If we confess our sins, he is faithful and just and will forgive us our sins and purify us from all unrighteousness.' Forgiveness is sweet, but a lack of awareness of this blessed grace will be debilitating for any believer. A particular sin or a past failure can so demoralize us that we become afraid to do anything for the Lord.

These verses in 1 John 1 remind us that forgiveness is only ours because the blood of Christ cleanses us from all sin. Dr Lloyd-Jones writes, 'So I am aware of my sinfulness and my unworthiness and my unrighteousness, I look to the blood of Jesus Christ, and I see there the forgiveness of God. I see the justice of God; I know that there God has forgiven and still forgives and will forgive. It is not that I am to make merchandise of the blood of Christ; not that I am to regard the blood of Christ as a cheap thing which allows me to continue in sin that grace may abound. No, it is that I can have this confidence that the death of Christ upon the cross is the propitiation for my sins — indeed, for the sins of the whole world — and that all my sins have been dealt with and are covered, are removed and banished there in him. Knowing thus the faithfulness and justice of God and the power of the blood of Christ to deliver me and to cleanse me from the guilt and stain of my sins, I can in confidence go forward, knowing that all is clear, my conscience has been cleansed and I can continue to walk with God.'[1]

The wisdom of the world quite rightly says that if you fall off a horse the best thing to do is to get straight back on. The grace of God said to Joshua, 'You made a mess of Ai; now go back there, and do it my way. Take the whole army, not just a token force, and go in the confidence that I have delivered the city to you.'

We are to learn from our defeats, and the prime lesson we must learn is that sin never pays. The failure is always our fault, but when the sin is dealt with, we can resume the struggle with confidence. The prophet Micah makes a very telling statement: 'Do not gloat over me, my enemy! Though I have fallen, I will rise' (Micah 7:8). That is not an expression of self-confidence but a remarkable trust in the grace of God. Every Christian must believe this, or we shall be paralysed by past failure and we shall fear to go again down the same road. How many of us would have given Ai a bypass? God will not allow that. 'Face the failure,' he says, 'but this time do it right.'

The battle

Jericho was conquered by a miracle, Ai by military tactics, but both methods were planned and ordained by God. Our business is not to dictate to the Almighty how he is to conduct the battle, but to fight according to his given plan. The common factor between Jericho and Ai is that God involved all the people — not just a select few. The Lord's people were called upon to act together. Each one did not have the same function in the battle, but they were all needed. All were important and supplemented each other. Likewise in the church, unless the pastor has the full backing of the elders and deacons he will be at a serious disadvantage. Unless the church members have confidence in the leaders, then little success will come. We are called upon, not to fight each other but to work with each other, and fight the enemies of God. This is why the New Testament puts such an emphasis upon the church — that is, upon the company of believers acting together.

One of the most tragic developments in recent years has been the way some evangelical Christians have tended to minimize the church. The result has been small groups each doing their own thing and launching into battle without any reference to the church. Sometimes the reason for this is frustration with the church's lack of vision and concern, but still we are called upon to act together and we must therefore work to achieve this.

The methods God used on the two occasions were different and so also were the instructions regarding plunder (compare 6:18-19 with 8:2). The lesson is important. Some Christians, reading in church history how God blessed remarkably in some revival, see the means God used and become very suspicious of anything that does not exactly match those means. Anything new is frowned upon and shunned. Clearly we are not to embrace everything with a naïve enthusiasm, but neither are we to ignore the fact that God's means of blessing can vary. We need to be very careful of not rejecting what God is doing simply because it is different.

An old Scottish preacher used to tell the story of the imagined meeting of the two men Christ had cured of blindness. They spoke enthusiastically of what the Lord had done for them and shared their experiences.

One said, 'How did you feel when Jesus put that mud on your eyes?'

His new friend was puzzled. 'He never put mud on my eyes,' he replied.

'Yes, he must have done if you were cured of your blindness. Don't you remember how he spat on the ground and made some mud and put it on your eyes?' said the man whose story is told in John 9.

'I tell you,' said the man we read about in Mark 8, 'he never put mud on my eyes.'

'If that is the case,' he was told, 'you were never healed. You must still be blind.'

The preacher's punch-line was: 'Immediately there were born two new denominations, the Mudites and the Antimudites!'

God's ways and provisions for his people can and do vary. They may be miraculous, or the divine use of our abilities and strengths. For example, Jesus fed two separate crowds of people miraculously with a few fish and loaves, yet on another occasion he sent his disciples to buy food (John 4:8). Today God has pledged himself to provide the needs of his people, whether they are spiritual or material. Is it possible that perhaps we do not see this pledge fulfilled because we refuse to accept that something is of the Lord simply because it is different from what we have known?

13.
If God be for us...?

Joshua 10:1-15

Joshua 10 relates one of the most remarkable miracles recorded in Scripture. By definition any miracle is remarkable, but for the sun to stand still seems more amazing than anything. Pink defines a miracle as a 'supernatural event brought about by a special act of divine providence, an extraordinary display of God's power. It is an event occurring in the natural world, which is apparent to the senses and of such a nature that it can be rationally attributed only to an immediate act of God.'[1]

Christianity is a supernatural faith; therefore we should not be surprised to read in the Bible of miracles. But these remarkable and exceptional acts of God that so baffle and defy human reason are not found everywhere in Scripture. John MacArthur writes, 'Most biblical miracles happened in three relatively brief periods of Bible history: in the days of Moses and Joshua, during the ministries of Elijah and Elisha, and in the time of Christ and the apostles. None of these periods lasted much more than a hundred years. Each of them saw a proliferation of miracles unheard of in other eras. Even during those three time periods, however, miracles were not exactly the order of the day. The miracles that happened involved men who were extraordinary messengers from God — Moses and Joshua, Elijah and Elisha, Jesus and the apostles.'[2] In Scripture there are a few other isolated incidents of the miraculous. But as MacArthur goes on to say, 'For the most part, however, supernatural events like those did not characterize God's dealings with his people.'

This has to be borne in mind today when you hear some Christians talk of miracles as if they are as common as a loaf of bread. I remember a few years ago seeing a large notice outside a church which read, 'Come in, there is a miracle waiting for you.' On the other hand there are Christians who do not believe that miracles are possible today. They argue that they finished at the end of the apostolic era. So even among Christians the subject can be contentious, but what every Bible-believing Christian has no doubt about is that the miracles recorded in Scripture actually happened.

Miracles remind man that he is not as clever as he thinks he is and they reveal the supreme glory and power of God. Once we accept the fact of a sovereign, omnipotent God, it is not difficult to believe in miracles.

Natural law

We are living in days of scepticism and arrogant unbelief, so miracles are rejected as impossible and contrary to the laws of nature. Particularly many of the Old Testament miracles, such as the sun standing still, are rejected as violating natural law. What this objection virtually amounts to is, at worst, a denial of the existence of God, and at best, a putting of the laws of nature in place of God. The so-called laws of nature are merely the means God has chosen to run the universe he has created. So the *Westminster Confession* states, 'God in his ordinary providence makes use of means, yet is free to work without, above or against them at his pleasure.' Nature is subject to God, not God to nature. To quote Pink again, 'Nature would cease to move were its Maker to withdraw his energy from it. It can no more operate itself than it could produce itself.'[3]

The battle for Gibeon

The battle for Gibeon was different from that of either Jericho or Ai, but what was evident in all the battles in Canaan was that 'Surely the LORD was fighting for Israel!' (10:14). At Gibeon the armies of five kings opposed Joshua. The victory was a combination of human strategy — the all-night march of the Israelites took the enemy by surprise — and the direct intervention of the Lord so that 'More of them died from the hailstones than were killed by the swords of the Israelites' (10:11).

Today Christians seem to have lost the concept of the Lord fighting for them. We have an image of a soft, sentimental God and a weak Jesus, gentle, meek and mild, so the God brought before us in Joshua 10 is a stranger. Yet this is the God of the whole of the Bible. David asks in Psalm 24, 'Who is this King of Glory?' The answer is: 'The LORD strong and mighty, the LORD mighty in battle.' The Jesus shown us in Revelation 19 is called 'the King of Kings and Lord of Lords' and this Jesus very powerfully and effectively fights for his people. We need such a Jesus because we ourselves are no match for the powers of darkness. We need such a Jesus to give us hope in the very bleak and depressing spiritual climate of our day.

The hailstones were a miracle and put the Amorites to rout. The enemy was on the run but the day was nearly over, and Joshua was afraid that they might escape in the darkness and re-muster to attack again. He was anxious to settle the battle once and for all, so he cried to the sun and moon to stand still until the fighting was over.

Joshua's prayer

The request to God to cause the sun and moon to stand still was made publicly in the presence of all the people. Why did Joshua pray for this remarkable thing? And how was it that he was confident enough to ask publicly? If ever a man went out on a limb Joshua did so with this prayer. As an experienced general he must have had several plans in mind to finish off the enemy — plans much more reasonable and possible than asking for the sun to stand still. So why this particular prayer?

Matthew Henry supplies some answers to these questions: 'No doubt, Joshua had an extraordinary impulse or impression upon his spirit, which he knew to be of divine origin, prompting him to desire that this miracle might be wrought upon this occasion, else it would have been presumption in him to desire or expect. The prayer would not have been granted by the divine power, if it had not been dictated by the divine grace... It cannot be imagined, however, that such a thing as this should have entered into his mind if God had not put it there... What God will give he inclines the hearts of his praying people to ask, and for what he will do he will be enquired of.'[4]

The faith of Joshua was remarkable, but it was a faith promoted by the awareness that God was with him. So he was not afraid that the Lord would shame him. He was confident that God would hear his cry because he was confident that God had inspired it. It was to the Almighty, the Creator of the sun and moon, that he looked, and he was not disappointed. Sceptics say that the sun never moves anyway — it is the earth that moves around the sun. True, but the same people will delight to talk of the beauty of a sunset — even though the sun does not move. The fact is that the light of day continued so that Joshua could continue the battle.

God is God. His ways are past understanding and the purpose of this miracle is not that we should understand how it could be, but that we should acknowledge God as the Almighty and worship him in awe and wonder. We should never forget that Christianity is a supernatural faith. If we take away the supernatural it becomes like any other religion. By supernatural we mean the demonstration of divine power and that God can break into the affairs of man any time he wishes and in any way that does not contradict his revealed will in Scripture. Today there is so much glib talk of divine power and ridiculous claims made of what God is supposed to have done. One effect of this has been to make believers wary of the supernatural and afraid of anything out of the ordinary. We have become comfortable with the ordinary and suspicious of anything new. To a degree this may be understandable, but it is very sad because the church has always needed the interventions of God and without them we are powerless.

14.
Accepting God's will

Joshua 13

Joshua was old; many battles had been fought but still large areas of Canaan had not been conquered. God did not tell Joshua that he was very old and therefore ought to think of retiring. Rather at this time the Lord gave him the toughest task of all — to divide the land among the tribes of Israel. This included areas of land not yet conquered. Those who have had the sad experience, following a death in the family, of the squabbles and bitterness that can develop when a will is administered are able to understand something of the difficulties facing Joshua. Here was the potential for that on a much more gigantic scale. It needed a man of Joshua's stature to organize it.

Old age can either be a hindrance or a blessing in the work of God. If an old man continually lives in the past, with no appreciation of what the Lord is doing now, he can be a painful hindrance. 'We never did it that way before', is not an unusual phrase to be heard from the lips of old elders and deacons. Often these are the last words of a dying church. Of course if the words are the fruit of wisdom and discernment in advising the church against worldly and unbiblical ways, they are to be listened to, but if they are simply nostalgia and a stubborn resistance to any change, they should be ignored.

Old age ought to produce wisdom in God's people; it is a great privilege for a church to have old saints in the fellowship who have walked long years with the Lord. Such men and women are not to be put on the scrap-heap, but treasured as gifts of God to his church. Joshua was certainly a treasure to be valued at a crucial time.

God's ways

Joshua probably would never have chosen that particular time to divide up the land. He may well have thought that there were more important things, like the final conquest of the land, to occupy him. But obviously God had different thoughts and God never does anything without a reason. His timings may seem to us to be strange on occasions, but he is never wrong. Joshua had learnt this lesson well and there was no argument from him. He just got on with the task. What seem to us to be urgent requirements all have to take second place to doing God's will in God's way at God's time.

The division was not vague or temporary, but detailed, with each tribe's boundary clearly defined. This is what God intended to be permanent for his people. But one could see problems arising. It was all right for some tribes whose inheritance had already been possessed, but what about a tribe being allotted land still occupied by the enemy? Potential problems do not mean that something is not God's will. Very often he ordains events so that the problems help to develop the character and deepen the faith of his people. To be promised as their inheritance land that was still possessed by the Canaanites stretched the faith of some tribes. On other tribes, who were given land already conquered, there was laid an obligation to help their brethren until all the tribes could live in peace. The division of the land did not mean the division of the nation. They were still one people, God's people, and they were to live as such.

Throughout the history of the church some Christians have always had it easier than others. To be a Christian in the 1960s in a Communist land was a totally different situation from being a Christian in the USA or Britain. And even within a country such as Britain there will always be differences among believers with regard to possessions and property. Such differences are inevitable, but they should not impair the essential unity of God's people. On the contrary, they ought to deepen our sense of responsibility for each other. What God has given us — homes, wealth, jobs — are given as trusts and not to be used exclusively for our self-indulgence, but for the glory of God and the well-being of his people.

This principle is worked out clearly in the New Testament in the emphasis put upon caring for brethren in material need (Acts 2:44-45; 4:32; 11:28-30). It is summed up by Paul in Romans 12:13: 'Share with God's people who are in need. Practise hospitality.' Peter says the same thing: 'Offer hospitality to one another without grumbling. Each one should use whatever gift he has received to serve others, faithfully administering God's grace in its various forms' (1 Peter 4:9-10).

The lot

The land was divided by lot (13:6, NKJV; 18:10,11). Exactly what form the lot took we do not know, but it was often used in the Old Testament and right up to Acts 1:26. Whatever it was, it was not a chancy gamble. The Israelites saw it as the revealing to them of God's will. There was no dividing up of the land into twelve equal parts. This would have appeared to be fair to human wisdom but God does not work like that. He gives as he wills. The lot system required everyone to accept contentedly what God gave them. There were no grounds for dispute or pleas of unfairness. The Israelites were taught to submit themselves to God's will and to accept gratefully what he gave them.

The lot system may appear to us to be very unspiritual but its value is in the belief that God decides and in the willingness to accept this. If God chooses, there are no mistakes. We may prefer to be 'led by the Spirit' — and who could argue against that? — but does this make us more willing to accept the difficult situations that come our way? Whatever our system of guidance, we need to be willing to surrender ourselves wholly to God's will and plead that he will choose our way for us. It is when we leave God out and lean on our own understanding that we bring trouble on ourselves. In almost any given situation our choice will be governed by what is the most profitable, or easiest, or most convenient way for us. In most of us there is a strong streak of self-will. So even if we pray sincerely for God's will to be done, all too often, if it comes to the crunch, it is our will that triumphs. The proof of that is the sad spiritual state of our churches. There is in most of us more of the Jonah than the Isaiah. Isaiah said, 'Here am I send me' — anywhere, to do anything. He was willing for God to choose. Jonah was also willing up to a point, but he had reservations, so when God said, 'Go to Nineveh,' he refused.

If we are honest we have to admit that we want to reserve the right to say no. But how we choose is indicative of where we are spiritually. Tozer says, 'A man is absent from church on Sunday morning. Where is he? If he is in hospital having his appendix removed his absence tells us nothing about him except that he is ill; but if he is out on the golf course, that tells us a lot. To go to the hospital is compulsory; to go to the golf course, voluntary. The man is free to choose and he chooses to play instead of to pray. His choice reveals what kind of man he is. Choices always do.'[1]

Such an attitude is always spiritually disastrous. Here is Tozer again: 'In every Christian's heart there is a cross and a throne, and the Christian is on the throne till he puts himself on the cross; if he refuses the cross he remains on the throne. Perhaps this is at the bottom of the backsliding and worldliness among gospel believers today... Our uncrucified flesh will rob us of purity of heart, Christlikeness of character, spiritual insight, fruitfulness; and more than all, it will hide from us the vision of God's face, that vision which has been the light of earth and will be the completeness of heaven.'[2]

Exceptions

When the land was divided there were two exceptions: first the Reubenites, Gadites and the half-tribe of Manasseh, and then the Levites.

We have seen that the two and a half tribes had their land on the east bank of the Jordan. Their land was outside the boundary of the promised land. They had asked for this and God had granted it, but it put them permanently on the borders of the rest of their brethren, not just geographically but also spiritually. It gave rise to the tension that arose in chapter 22 and almost led to a civil war. Even worse, it led to the half-tribe of Manasseh becoming 'unfaithful to the God of their fathers' so that they 'prostituted themselves to the gods of the peoples of the land, whom God had destroyed before them' (1 Chr. 5:25). What God wills for his people and what he allows them to have are not always the same thing. It is not unusual to hear Christians say, 'If God does not want me to have it, he will not give it to me.' This is a dangerous and unscriptural argument, as Psalm 106:15 reminds us: 'He gave them their request, but sent leanness into their soul' (NKJV). The two and a half tribes would have been better off if they had simply accepted that God's will for them, like the rest of their brethren, was inside the promised land.

The Levites had no land for their inheritance because the Lord himself was their inheritance (Deut. 18:2). God did not want them to be concerned about land, but to concentrate on their crucial ministry of being priests for all the people. Their material needs were to be met from the offerings and sacrifices made to the Lord. As well as this the Levites were given forty-eight towns and pasture-lands. These cities were taken from all the tribes as their contribution to the spiritual ministry God had ordained for them. Also it spread the Levites throughout the nation so that their ministry was known and experienced everywhere.

15.
Avoiding apathy

Joshua 18:1-10

Some time after the beginning of the division of the land, seven tribes had still not received their inheritance (18:2). It is clear from verse 3 that this was due to the slackness of the people. Somehow or other these tribes had become indifferent to the promised blessing of God and made no effort to receive it. Joshua had to rebuke them: 'How long will you wait before you begin to take possession of the land that the LORD, the God of your fathers, has given you?'

It seems inconceivable that, after forty years in the wilderness and five years of fighting, such an indolent spirit should exist. We may have expected them to be keen to receive their land and enjoy its blessings. This slackness was true of seven tribes — over half of the nation.

Too easily satisfied

One reason for the slackness could have been that they were now having things relatively easy compared with years gone by. They were not meeting too much opposition and they had become satisfied with their present condition. The spoil won in past battles enabled them to live comfortably and they were not too concerned about the future. If asked they would have agreed that they ought to be seeking their inheritance, but there was no hurry. They were not desperate and had no great incentive to seek it. They were enjoying their peace and quiet and did not want to be disturbed.

The picture is very much like modern evangelical Christianity. We are saved by grace and have known something of God's mercies and blessings. We can read in Scripture of our rich spiritual inheritance, but we are stagnant and indolent. Instead of going on with Christ we have become comfortable and nothing is allowed to disturb our spiritual slackness. No effort is made to mortify our lusts and no serious energy put into seeking holiness. Our Christian life just drifts, with no direction and no purpose. Our problem is that we are satisfied with being saved. It may be objected, 'What is wrong with that?' Everything! It is wrong to be satisfied with being a babe in Christ and never wanting to grow. It is like a man being saved from drowning, pulled out of the sea, brought to the safety of the beach, and then spending the rest of his life making sand-castles. To these Christians God says, 'How long will you be slack and not claim all the blessings I have for you in Christ?'

Some will have doctrinal excuses for their slackness and claim that God will bless us in his time, and it is not for us to seek blessings. Pink laments, 'Alas, how hyper-Calvinists have sought to excuse their apathy by perverting and sheltering behind the divine decrees! How fearfully deceitful is the human heart in persuading not a few that they are displaying a commendable spirit of humility and meekness in "waiting God's time" before they act, when instead they are guilty of shirking their duty. There is a terrible amount of humbuggery under a seemingly pious guise. There is no unwillingness on God's part to give: the unwillingness to seek and take is always on our side. Then let us be honest, and place the blame where it belongs.'[1]

Other Christians do not even have a pious-sounding excuse. They mourn about the moral and spiritual state of the nation, but the truth is that they are happy as they are. They are content with believing the right doctrines but knowing nothing of the power of the Holy Spirit. Correct doctrine, though crucial, is no substitute for the presence and power of God. Like the seven tribes we know that we have an inheritance but we are not too bothered about claiming it.

Our inheritance

God brought the Israelites out of the slavery of Egypt and into the promised land so that they could live in the place he had provided for them and enjoy the abundant fruit of a land flowing with milk and honey. In the same way God has saved us from the slavery of sin and put us 'in Christ'. He wants us to live our lives in the presence of the living Christ and to enjoy all that the Holy Spirit wants to give us here and now. To be 'in Christ' is a theological fact true of all the redeemed, but sadly what is not true is that all the redeemed are living in obedience and submission to the lordship of Christ. Consequently we know very little of the power and influence of the Holy Spirit in our lives and in our churches.

It is God's command that all Christians should be filled with the Spirit (Eph. 5:18). It is God's will that all Christians should produce the fruit of the Spirit in their lives (Gal. 5:22). If these are not true of us then we have not obtained what we were saved for. We can debate all day about the doctrine of the Holy Spirit, but the simple statement of Jesus in Luke 11:13 remains true: 'How much more will your Father in heaven give the Holy Spirit to those who ask him!' The parable in Luke 11 tells of a man who had an unexpected guest and had nothing to give him to eat. Most ladies have probably experienced at some time the embarrassment of this kind of situation, and certainly all believers will have recognized the poverty of our spiritual resources to meet the needs all around us. So what do we do? We go to a friend who we know has the resources — we go to Christ. In the parable the friend's answer — 'Don't bother me. It's late. We are all in bed' — is understandable and reasonable. But reasonableness is no answer to a desperate man, and this man is desperate. He wants bread now, not tomorrow. So he bangs on the door and is shameless in his persistence. Jesus says it is this persistence that is rewarded.

Persistence is the product of desperation; desperation comes from recognition of our own miserable resources and an overwhelming desire to give to others what they need.

Jesus applies the parable to asking God for the Holy Spirit. When we ask for the Spirit, what are we asking for? Is it for tongues and the power to do miracles, or is it for holiness and the ability to witness? Surely it must be to enable us to live our lives by the Spirit's power in such a way as to please God and honour the Lord Jesus Christ. This will enable us to be light in a world of darkness and chaos. We need to be filled with the Spirit, according to Ephesians 5, not to do remarkable things, but to live the normal Christian life and to be a good husband, wife, parent and worker. We need to exhibit the fruit of the Spirit, according to Galatians 5, in order to show we belong to Christ.

Our inheritance is to know and enjoy the Lord Jesus Christ in all his fulness and to experience all that he has for us in this life as well as the future glory of heaven. The problem, says Tozer, is that 'Many Christians want to be filled, but their desire is a vague romantic kind of thing hardly worthy to be called desire. They have almost no knowledge of what it will cost them to realize it.'² Tozer then goes on to say, 'Are you sure you want to be filled with a Spirit who, though he is like Jesus in his gentleness and love, will nevertheless demand to be Lord of your life? ... If the Spirit takes charge of your life he will expect unquestioning obedience in everything... He may strip you of many of those border-line pleasures which other Christians enjoy but which are to you a source of refined evil. Through it all he will enfold you in a love so vast, so mighty, so all-embracing, so wondrous that your very losses will seem like gains and your small pains like pleasures.'

How long?

Joshua said to Israel, 'How long will you be satisfied with less than God has for you?' He could well say to us, 'How long will you be satisfied with bread and jam when there is a banquet available for you?' Joshua's answer to the slackness of his people was to get them 'to make a survey of the land and write a description of it' (18:4). If we were to make a spiritual and moral survey of our land what would we find? From the top to the bottom, from the royal palace to the poorest hovel, God is a stranger. Our churches are empty, our governments pass bills that are diametrically opposed to what the Bible teaches, the vast majority of those under the age of thirty have never been to a Sunday School; abortion, suicide, divorce, crime, every abuse are all on the increase.

The scene is frightening and exposes the indolent, slack attitude in the church as inexcusable. There is much to be done, but we cannot do it in our own strength. We need all that God has promised us in Scripture. May the Lord grant us an urgent and desperate seeking after the power and presence of the Holy Spirit so that we may exalt Jesus in our land. Our prayer needs to be that of Psalm 85:

Will you not revive us again,
>   that your people may rejoice in you? …
>   that his glory may dwell in our land

(vv. 6,9).

16.
Christi is our refuge

Joshua 20

In Joshua 20 we are given the story of the setting up of six cities of refuge. Details of the purpose of these cities have been given previously in Numbers 35 and Deuteronomy 19, but now they are actually established. The cities were not Joshua's idea but God's, and speak to us profoundly of both the justice and mercy of the Lord.

Long before the Mosaic law, before there was even a Jewish nation, God had declared in Genesis 9:6:

Whoever sheds the blood of man,
    by man shall his blood be shed;
for in the image of God
    has God made man.

In other words, God instituted capital punishment as the penalty for murder, but he also made a clear distinction between wilful murder and accidental manslaughter (Deut. 19:4-7). It was to cover the killing 'without malice aforethought' that God set up the cities of refuge.

Justice and mercy

In the time of Joshua the law said that if a man was killed, his next of kin had the right to take revenge. He was called 'the avenger of blood'. In a time when there were no police forces this arrangement saw to it that no one took murder lightly, but it could also lead to injustice. The avenger of blood, in his anger and bitterness at the death of a loved one, might not care whether the killing was intentional or not. All he was concerned about was vengeance. It was to meet this situation that God established the six cities. They sought to maintain justice and at the same time to exercise mercy.

If the innocent killer fled to one of these cities he was safe. The cities were spread evenly around the country so that at least one of them would be accessible. Roads were built to the cities to help the person fleeing. Jewish law tells us that these roads had to be well maintained and signposted, and that one day a year the signposts were checked to see that the name *Miklac* (refuge), was clear and legible. Everything was done to help the fleeing man.

Once in the city of refuge, he had to state his case before the elders of that city. If they decided he was guilty of an accidental killing but not of murder, he was allowed to stay. A trial took place, so the man was subject to reasonable argument and evidence, not the rage of the avenger of blood. Once all this was done satisfactorily he could stay in the city and live in peace. If he left the city he would still have to face the avenger of blood, but at the death of the high priest he could leave the city and return to his home and the avenger of blood could not touch him.

A pattern and a contrast

This Old Testament practice sets before us both a pattern of, and a number of contrasts with, our salvation in Christ. The contrast is that there is no question of whether our sin is accidental or deliberate: we are all guilty. Sin is not something that is the result of a set of unfortunate circumstances. Our nature is sinful and we commit sins because our hearts are sinful. This is a very real problem.

This has always been the major problem facing society, and thousands of years of history and scientific progress have not changed the situation. It is man's selfishness and greed that cause many to be hungry, produce broken homes and create a drug problem. Every known social problem can be traced back to the fact that man in his sin has rejected God's way. Man may be a stone-age sinner or a twenty-first-century space-age sinner, but sinner he is, and sin never produces anything but misery.

There is no human remedy for sin. Moral reform and social laws may curb man's sinful nature for a while, but they cannot change it. The only remedy is God's remedy. The Lord sent his Son into the world to atone for our sin. This involved Jesus taking the guilt of our sin upon himself and paying the punishment the law of God demanded. He died on the cross as a propitiation for our sin. He faced the wrath of God instead of us and thus provided for guilty sinners a free and full salvation. He became our place of safety, our refuge from the consequence of our sin. When we come to him for forgiveness there is no need for a trial to see whether or not we are guilty. That is settled because all have sinned and we are condemned already. Jesus is the refuge for guilty sinners who deserve death and hell. Only divine grace could provide such a salvation.

Whereas there were six cities of refuge, there is for us only one Saviour. Jesus is unique and God offers no alternative to him. If a sinner wants salvation there is only one Saviour to go to. The Old Testament killer fleeing for his life could not decide to go to Jerusalem or Bethlehem for refuge. The choice was not his. God had ordained where refuge was to be found and it was in one of these six cities or nowhere. In the same way God has ordained that 'Salvation is found in no one else, for there is no other name under heaven given to men by which we must be saved' (Acts 4:12).

Another contrast is seen in the function of the high priest. When he died the Old Testament fugitive could leave the city in safety, but Christ our High Priest will never die. Our salvation is secure because of his continuing priesthood: 'But because Jesus lives for ever, he has a permanent priesthood. Therefore he is able to save completely those who come to God through him, because he always lives to intercede for them' (Heb. 7:24-25).

So there are several contrasts — but the pattern, or picture, is thrilling. First of all, the way to the cities of refuge was plainly signposted and kept in good repair. No refugee could argue that he did not know the way, or could not find the place of safety. The gospel is basically a very simple and uncomplicated message that even a child can understand. After 2,000 years it still says the same thing. It is true that there have been many attempts to corrupt its message, and thus send sinners in the wrong direction, but God has protected his truth. If a man truly wants to find the way of salvation, even though the road is narrow, it is clear. Jesus said, 'I am the way.'

God has provided a salvation for guilty sinners, but he demands that we seek the Lord and come to him in repentance and faith. We must flee to Christ, says Hebrews 6:18: 'we who have fled to take hold of the hope offered to us'. In other words, when the sinner flees to Christ for refuge he is safe from the divine avenger of blood. Paul tells us in Romans, 'Since we have now been justified by his blood, how much more shall we be saved from God's wrath through him!' (Rom. 5:9), and he also says, 'Therefore, there is now no condemnation for those who are in Christ Jesus' (Rom. 8:1). Regardless of what sin he has committed, there is for the repentant sinner a full salvation in Jesus Christ.

There are some people who seem to take a delight in teaching that the God of the Old Testament was a different God from the one Jesus revealed in the Gospels. They say the Old Testament God was a bloodthirsty, revenge-taking, merciless

God, totally unlike the God of love we see in the teaching of Jesus. This could not be more wrong because in all ages God has tempered his justice with mercy. The cities of refuge are an example of the mercy and grace of God. Our God is a God of mercy, love and grace. That does not mean that he will tolerate sin. He is holy, and his holiness demands that sin is dealt with, but in mercy God provides for the guilty sinner a refuge.

17.
Thinking about what we do

Joshua 22

A number of years had passed since Israel had crossed Jordan and entered the promised land. There were still parts of the land unconquered but by and large Canaan was theirs. The nation was now settling down to the business of ordinary life.

We have made several allusions to the two and a half tribes who had their land on the east bank of Jordan; now, here in chapter 22, they are referred to once again. Their obligation to fight with the other tribes until the land was subdued was now over and Joshua gave them permission to return to their families and lands. He did so with a glowing tribute to their faithfulness. They had done their duty both to the Lord and to their fellow Israelites. Their promise had been kept and they parted on the warmest possible terms. Unfortunately this was not to last. Soon Joshua and the other tribes were preparing to make war on them and it was all the result of a silly misunderstanding that could easily have been avoided.

Another memorial

When the Reubenites, Gadites and the half tribe of Manasseh arrived at their land the first thing they did was to make what the NIV calls 'an imposing altar', and the NKJV refers to as 'a great impressive altar' (22:10). The Israelites as a nation seemed to delight in making memorials in some shape or form. This was now the eighth since they crossed the Jordan. It is true that some were at God's command but not all, and certainly not this one. The reason for building was commendable. They wanted it to be a reminder to following generations that they were God's people. Whether this was the best way to do this is open to doubt. Their own devotion and faithfulness, their God-centred worship and God-honouring lives would have done it much better. Wiersbe says, 'It's unfortunate when believers have to resort to artificial means to let people know they're God's people. In recent years we've seen a spate of "religious" bumper stickers, jewellery and other items (including mirrors and combs with Bible verses on them), all of which are supposed to help identify the owners with Jesus Christ. While these things might occasionally open doors of opportunity for witness, how much better it would be if our Spirit-led conduct and speech made the lost sit up and take notice.'[1]

Such a reminder was needed because they were not actually in the promised land. Years before, in Numbers 32, they had made their decision, based on material, not spiritual reasons, as to where they wanted to live. It would have been better if they had thought out the spiritual consequences of that decision then rather than now in Joshua 22. Every decision a Christian makes will have spiritual consequences sooner or later. Responsible living means that we will think through our choices and try to anticipate all eventualities. If we choose to take a job in an area where there is no Bible-believing church to attend, then the consequences a few years later for our children, as well as for our own spiritual vitality, will be obvious. Of course there will always be matters that it is impossible to anticipate, but where we can we should. Building altars is no substitute for being in the right place.

Thinking through our actions also means trying to anticipate how they will affect other believers. The two and half
tribes should have realized that their imposing altar would be
a real problem for the tribes on the west bank. The whole
action, their not thinking through the consequences, and the
other tribes jumping to the wrong conclusion, was a recipe for
disaster. In a sense both parties were acting out of proper
motives. The two and a half tribes were concerned to show
they belonged to God's people and the other tribes were concerned for the purity of worship (v. 19). They had at least
learned the lesson of Achan well enough to know that God
would not stand by idly if his people sinned (v. 20).

Woolly thinking

Though their motives were right the thinking of the two and a
half tribes was confused and woolly. They knew from Deuteronomy 12:5-7 that God had ordained that the only altar for
worship was to be at Shiloh. Their altar was not intended for
sacrifice but to remind the children of the other tribes in the
promised land, as well as their own, that they were all one
people. As we have seen, this was a strange way of doing so.
And it is a strange argument they use in verse 25: 'Your descendants might cause ours to stop fearing the LORD.' If anything would cause their children to stop fearing the Lord it
would be their choice to live separate from their brethren. They
justify this by saying, 'The LORD has made the Jordan a boundary between us and you' (22:24).

How easy it is to impose upon our decisions the stamp of
divine approval! It was they, not God, who made Jordan a
barrier between them and their brethren. Woolly thinking can
soon become dishonest thinking. And it is not long before we

even believe our distorted logic. 'The Lord knows our hearts,' they said. The problem was, did they know their own hearts? There is nothing more dangerous than a Christian who has convinced himself that wrong is right; who is convinced that his actions, though done for all sorts of wrong reasons, are approved by God. Such folk can be deadly in a church as with pious language they blame others for problems they themselves have caused.

The problem with woolly thinking is that it does not see that it is woolly. To the person concerned it all seems so clear and obvious. Perhaps we had all better learn that there are occasions when a simple word of explanation before an action can defuse potential problems. The two and a half tribes seem to have been surprised that their fellow Israelites should have misinterpreted their action, but a little forethought on their part, and a short delay in building the altar while they sent an explanation to their brethren, would have removed all the tension and threats of war.

Jumping to conclusions

If the two and a half tribes were wrong, then so too were the rest of the Israelites. They heard about the altar and immediately jumped to the wrong conclusion. Their thinking was that an altar could only mean one thing, and that was sacrifice. They knew that sacrifice outside of God's ordained place was sin; therefore this was sinful.

Their brethren's action may have been stupid but it was not sinful. How often are we all caught out like this? We conclude that there can be only one explanation for a certain action, but we are wrong and there is another explanation. The sad thing is that the Israelites were quick to attribute the worst possible motives to brethren upon whom only very recently they had heaped praise. And in no time they were prepared to go to war with them.

Are we like this? What do you do when you hear that a Christian whom you have known and respected has done or said some terrible thing? Do you immediately accept what you hear to be the truth, or do you refuse to believe it until you have spoken to that Christian and heard his explanation?

How often do we say to someone, 'I heard such and such a thing about Mr X. I don't know if it is true, but...'? If we do not know whether it is true then we ought to be quiet. Many a fine Christian has had his reputation ruined by such gossip. Many a faithful pastor's ministry has been seriously undermined by such irresponsible talk.

Innocent actions can be misconstrued, exaggerated and blown up out of all proportion. Sometimes we misrepresent an action of a fellow believer because we do not like that person and are only too glad for an opportunity to criticize. That is evil and wicked. Sometimes we misrepresent an action because we disagree with it. That is dishonest because the motives can be right even when the action is wrong.

The Israelites were too quick to misconstrue and much too quick to be ready to fight, but we must pay tribute to them that before they did anything they sent representatives to talk with their brethren. When they came face to face and talked the whole business through the problems were resolved.

Our churches

How many 'wars' in the local church could be avoided if we all followed the New Testament commands on how to deal with disputes:

Therefore, as God's chosen people, holy and dearly loved, clothe yourselves with compassion, kindness, humility, gentleness and patience. Bear with each other and forgive whatever grievances you may have against one another. Forgive as the Lord forgave you. And over all these virtues put on love, which binds them all together in perfect unity (Col. 3:12-14).

Brothers, do not slander one another. Anyone who speaks against his brother or judges him speaks against the law and judges it. When you judge the law, you are not keeping it, but sitting in judgement on it (James 4:11).

Finally, all of you, live in harmony with one another; be sympathetic, love as brothers, be compassionate and humble. Do not repay evil with evil or insult with insult, but with blessing, because to this you were called so that you may inherit a blessing (1 Peter 3:8-9).

18.
Being totally committed to God

Joshua 23-24

Joshua was now very old and he knew that his leadership of Israel would not go on much longer. In the last two chapters he calls the nation together to address them for the final time. He challenges them to be faithful to God and at the same time he reminds them of the faithfulness of God to them. Without the intervention of God Israel would still have been in Egypt. Everything that had happened to them since the exodus — the hardships and the blessings — was all a direct result of their relationship to God. Being God's people was not a hobby they could take up and put down whenever they fancied. It was what they were and affected everything they did. The only explanation for Israel was God.

Israel's God

Joshua is doing much the same thing that the aged Peter did at the end of his life: 'So I will always remind you of these things, even though you know them and are firmly established in the truth you now have. I think it is right to refresh your memory as long as I live in the tent of this body, because I know that I will soon put it aside, as our Lord Jesus Christ has made clear to me. And I will make every effort to see that after my departure you will always be able to remember these things' (2 Peter

1:12-15). Peter wrote to remind Christians of the riches of their inheritance in Christ. Joshua does much the same thing.

Over and over again he mentions 'the LORD your God'. The Hebrew word for 'LORD' is Jehovah and emphasizes that God is the I AM. It was the name by which God chose to reveal himself to Moses in Exodus 6. It emphasizes the unchangeable nature of God: the one without beginning or end, the incomparable God. To have such a God gives the people security and a guaranteed future. Generation after generation will never outlive this God. He will never become obsolete or irrelevant. He is Jehovah.

He is also *Elohim,* the Hebrew word for God. This is the name for God which occurs nearly thirty times in Genesis 1. It tells of God's creative power and unchallengeable omnipotence. The two names, Jehovah and *Elohim,* 'the LORD your God', speak of divine grace and divine power working for them.

They needed to be reminded of this and so do we as Christians because this is our God. He is a God of grace; if it were not for this we could never know him. Salvation is all of grace; it requires divine power to break the hold of Satan on our lives. Grace is not a way of helping sinners to be saved; it is God's way of salvation. In other words, grace is not given to aid or assist us; it is the power of God to save us. Grace and power are an invincible combination. What an enormous privilege we have to be Christians and to have such a God to worship and serve! The only explanation for the Christian church is God.

Back to the Book

In chapter 23:6-8 Joshua brings the people back to the book he had exhorted them to obey in chapter 1. The message of the Book with regard to our relationship to God has not changed from Joshua's time right up to the New Testament, and it is still applicable today. The Book says no compromise with the world: 'Do not associate with these nations that remain among you; do not invoke the names of their gods or swear by them. You must not serve them or bow down to them' (23:7). The New Testament says, 'Do not be yoked together with unbelievers. For what do righteousness and wickedness have in common? Or what fellowship can light have with darkness? What harmony is there between Christ and Belial? What does a believer have in common with an unbeliever?' (2 Cor. 6:14-15).

The reason for such commands is clear. It has all to do with the worship of the one true God. If believers want to live like unbelievers, and worship like them, let them join with such people, but they cannot have it both ways. Faithfulness to God is impossible if we are in spiritual alliance with unbelievers. God's way is one of no compromise: 'Throw away the foreign gods that are among you and yield your hearts to the LORD, the God of Israel' (24:23).

Such a commitment is not a matter of words alone. The Israelites said, 'We too will serve the LORD, because he is our God.' Joshua replied that it is not as easy as that: 'You are not able to serve the LORD' (24:18,19). Why not? Because he is a holy God, a jealous God, and will not share the hearts of his people with gods which are the creation of the minds and hearts of men.

The Book also demands that we are to 'be very careful to love the LORD [your] God' (23:11). This is the same message from the lips of Joshua that was to come from the lips of Jesus. Love for God is not just a sentimental, emotional feeling; it is the result of God's loving us. John reminds us that 'We love [him] because he first loved us' (1 John 4:19). This is not only a New Testament truth but also the experience of all the Old

Testament saints. They would have been amazed at the suggestion that their God demonstrated only wrath and not love. Had he not made with them a covenant of love? (Neh. 9:32). Therefore his love for them was everlasting (Jer. 31:3), great (Ps. 89:1) and unfailing (Ps. 6:4). They delighted in God's love and joined with David to 'Give thanks to the LORD, for he is good; his love endures for ever' (1 Chr. 16:34). They knew that God loved them and that because of this they were precious to him and honoured in his sight (Isa. 43:4).

It was the reality of God's love that gave authority to Joshua's command that they should be very careful to love God. He had earned their love but, such is the depravity of human nature, he does not always get it, so there is the need for man to be careful in this matter. This reminds us that love is not a spontaneous emotion but a response of the mind and will to all that God has done for us. This is why Jesus commands us to love. You cannot command a spontaneous emotion but you can command a reasonable response of the mind and will.

Love for God, as far as Joshua is concerned, is shown in obedience to him. This is exactly how Jesus defines it in John 14:23: 'If anyone loves me, he will obey my teaching.' John tells us that love is not a matter of words but of action and truth (1 John 3:18). For Joshua this action and truth meant an uncompromising commitment to the Lord alone. There could be no room for other gods. This is the message of the Bible all the way through its unfolding revelation. The devastating effects of ignoring it are spelt out by Joshua in 23:12-13 and in the New Testament in Galatians 1:6-9.

Lessons from history

The last chapter of Joshua, though known as his farewell speech, is really a word from the Lord: 'This is what the LORD, the God of Israel, says...' The first words of God through his servant Joshua are 'Long ago', and from there the history of God's dealings with Israel is recounted. Moses did the same in Deuteronomy 26 as he anticipated entry into the promised land. Stephen used the same approach in Acts 7 before the Sanhedrin to show the rebellion of Israel against the Lord that reached its climax in the rejection of the Messiah.

History has great lessons for God's people. Its shows us man's failure, but the greatest lesson is God's faithfulness. The progress of Israel at the end of Joshua's life was due to one thing only: 'I brought you to the land' (24:8). The Lord's work is always thrilling to see and a source of great encouragement for the Christian. Joshua reminds us of the most unlikely beginning of God's work. The Lord started with a pagan idolater named Abraham. We can see the same pattern throughout history. In the New Testament God took a Christ-hating Pharisee named Saul of Tarsus. In the great spiritual darkness of the sixteenth century he chose a Roman Catholic monk called Martin Luther. In the eighteenth century he used an innkeeper's son from Gloucester and, through George Whitefield and the intellectual, rather aloof, John Wesley, set England alight with the Methodists' Revival. During the nineteenth century God raised up a teenage preacher who never went to theological college, and Charles Spurgeon still speaks to us today through the printed page.

We need to remember the activity of God because if we forget we shall find ourselves in all sorts of trouble. God works in the way he does in order to elevate his own glory and show us that we need him above everything else. God's choices were not perfect men, and Abraham, Luther, Whitefield and the others all made mistakes, but because they were God's men blessings came through them to the church. Next to his own glory, God's great desire is for the good of his people. Joshua labours this point. Problems come, he says, enemies arise, but

God deals with them all. What an encouragement that is for us! History proves that God reigns. The Christian church would have been dead and buried centuries ago if this were not true.

Joshua reviews the grace and goodness of God in the past in order to appeal to the hearts and minds of the people for a true love for God. Nothing moves the heart like a recollection of God's grace to us in our times of need. This leads up to Joshua's punch-line: 'Choose for yourselves this day whom you will serve' (24:15).

Total commitment

Half-hearted, insipid Christianity is an insult to God. Joshua calls for a total commitment based on fear and respect for God, and faithfulness in service. In order to produce this quality of service there must be a putting away of other gods. Israel was still being influenced by gods of the past, gods their forefathers had worshipped in Egypt. Literally for them Joshua's command meant destroying idols. For us it means putting out of our lives things that challenge the authority of God in our affections and desires.

This is what it means to serve the Lord, but then Joshua adds, 'If this seems undesirable to you, if you think such demands are too much, too restrictive, and you are unwilling to give God what he deserves, then choose which gods you are going to serve. Be honest,' he says. 'If you are not prepared to serve God as he commands then stop pretending and stop living a lie. Come out openly and say you are going to serve materialism, worldliness, prosperity and all the gods of the modern age. If these are the gods who have the love of your heart, then say so, but you cannot have it both ways. It is either the Lord God or these other gods.'

Such straight talking must have shocked these people for they responded with some indignation: 'Far be it for us to forsake the LORD to serve other gods' (24:16).

This does not satisfy Joshua and he responds: 'You are not able to serve the LORD. He is a holy God; he is a jealous God. He will not forgive your rebellion and your sins' (24:19). Joshua was not being hard or unreasonable. He was simply facing the Israelites with the reality of the holiness of God. They had been accused of putting other things before God and they had not denied it. They could not because it was true, but neither had they admitted it or shown any repentance. As long as that attitude continued they could not serve God and the warning of verse 20 was real: 'If you forsake the LORD and serve foreign gods, he will turn and bring disaster on you and make an end of you, after he has been good to you.'

Aghast at the thought of this they cried out, 'No! We will serve the Lord.'

Joshua's reply was: 'Let's see the evidence of this proclamation; yield your hearts to God.'

Joshua's words were uncompromising, but they were needed, and they are still needed today. In these days of evangelical fence-sitters who want to have one foot in the church and one foot in the world, the call has to be: 'You can't have it both ways.' The danger of insipid Christianity is that it spreads. Joshua knew this and so declared unequivocally his own position: 'But as for me and my household, we will serve the LORD' (24:15). The church today desperately needs men and women of the same sanctified determination.

Dale Ralph Davis writes, 'It is all or nothing. Israel must give themselves completely to Yahweh or not at all. It is the hog's dilemma in that hackneyed hog and hen story. Both hen and hog were walking past a church and noted the pastor's sermon title on the outside bulletin board. It read: "What can we do to help the poor?" As hogs and hens are wont to do, they entered into earnest conversation over the question as they continued on their way. At last, the hen was smitten with a bright idea: "I've got it," she cackled, "we can help the poor by giving them a ham and eggs breakfast!" "Oh no you don't," shot back the hog, "for you, that only means a contribution, but for me, it means total commitment." The old sow was right. That is Joshua's point — there can be no chicken's way out, but Israel must go the whole hog (if one may so speak) for Yahweh. No compromise on this point. They must consider whose slaves they will be.'[1]

Total commitment means just that. It allows no rivals to the Lord Jesus Christ into the heart and mind. When rivals seek to get in they are immediately shown the door. It is the only way to live the Christian life in an unbelieving world. This is not simply a matter of will-power; if it was, then nearly all of us would fail miserably. This is the outworking of grace in the Christian's life. It is because we are *in Christ* that God calls upon us to be *like Christ*. One would be impossible without the other. Sanctification is possible only when justification is a reality. But when we are justified it should, and must, lead to the fruits of sanctification being seen in our lives. Total commitment is the sanctified life of the Christian delighting in service of the Lord he, or she, loves and adores.

Joshua saw his God as worthy of all he could give. So too did Paul: 'But whatever was to my profit I now consider loss for the sake of Christ. What is more, I consider everything a loss compared to the surpassing greatness of knowing Christ Jesus my Lord, for whose sake I have lost all things. I consider them rubbish that I may gain Christ' (Phil. 3:8). Commenting on these verses, James Montgomery Boice says, 'That is the work of God in a man's heart. Paul came to the point where he opened his ledger book. And after he had looked at all of the things that he had accumulated by inheritance and by his efforts, he reflected that these things had actually kept him from Christ. He then took the entire list and placed it where it belonged — under the list of liabilities. He called it "loss". And under assets he wrote, "Jesus Christ alone." [2]

When we evaluate the worth of our lives only in terms of how they please Christ, then, by the power of the Holy Spirit, we are able to commit our lives to God and serve him as he desires and deserves.

Notes

Chapter 1 — Blessings don't come easily
1. John Calvin, *Commentary,* Baker, 1979 p.xix.
2. Matthew Henry, *Commentary on the Whole Bible,* Frederick Westley & Davies, 1836, vol. 1, p.519.

Chapter 2 — Focusing on God
1. A. W. Pink, *Gleanings in Joshua,* Moody Press, 1964, p.34.

Chapter 3 — Knowing God's will
1. D. Martyn Lloyd-Jones, *Authority,* IVP, 1958, p.60.
2. Henry, *Commentary,* p.520.

Chapter 4 — God expects total obedience
1. Warren Wiersbe, *Be Strong,* Chariot Victor, Cook Communications, 1997, p.29.
2. As above, p.30.
3. Charles Spurgeon, *Treasury of David,* Marshall, Morgan & Scott, 1950, vol. 3, p.256.

Chapter 5 — Welcoming sinners
1. R. T. Kendall, *Who by Faith,* Hodder, 1981, p.180.
2. Calvin, *Commentary,* p.47.
3. Wiersbe, *Be Strong,* p.37.
4. Pink, *Gleanings in Joshua,* p.64.
5. Dale Ralph Davis, *No Falling Words,* Baker, 1996, p.29.

Chapter 6 — Learning to trust God
1. Eifion Evans, *When He is Come,* Evangelical Movement of Wales, 1959, p.57.
2. Pink, *Gleanings in Joshua,* p.79.

Chapter 7 — Remembering what God has done
1. Wiersbe, *Be Strong,* p.55.
2. Arnold Dallimore, *Life of George Whitefield,* Banner of Truth, 1980, vol. 2, p.353.

Chapter 8 — We belong to God
1. Davis, *No Falling Words,* p.46.
2. Wiersbe, *Be Strong,* p.589.
3. D. Martyn Lloyd-Jones, *The Righteous Judgement of God,* Banner of Truth, 1989, p.154.
4. Davis, *No Falling Words,* p.49.

Chapter 9 — The Lord is our Captain
1. Wiersbe, *Be Strong,* p.65.
2. C. H. Spurgeon, *Encyclopaedia of Sermons,* PC Bible, 'Joshua's Vision'.

Chapter 10 — God will fight the battle
1. H. C. Leupold, *Exposition of Genesis,* Evangelical Press, 1972, p.486.
2. Davis, *No Falling Words,* p.52.
3. Evans, *When He is Come,* p.45.

Chapter 11 — Sin has consequences
1. Henry, *Commentary,* p.538.
2. Davis, *No Falling Words,* p.64.
3. Wiersbe, *Be Strong,* p.93.

Chapter 12 — Recovering from discouragements
1. D. Martyn Lloyd-Jones, *Fellowship with God,* Crossway, 1993, vol. 1, p.145.

Chapter 13 — If God be for us...?
1. Pink, *Gleanings in Joshua,* p.278.
2. John MacArthur, *Charismatic Chaos,* Zondervan, 1992, p.112.
3. Pink, *Gleanings in Joshua,* p.278.
4. Henry, *Commentary,* p. 552.

Chapter 14 — Accepting God's will
1. A. W. Tozer, *Man the Dwelling-Place of God,* Christian Publications, 1966, p.158.
2. A. W. Tozer, *The Root of the Righteous,* Christian Publications, 1955, p.66.

Chapter 15 — Avoiding apathy
1. Pink, *Gleanings in Joshua,* p.367.
2. Tozer, *The Divine Conquest,* Marshall, Morgan & Scott, 1964 p.122.

Chapter 17 — Thinking about what we do
1. Wiersbe, *Be Strong,* p.139.

Chapter 18 — Being totally committed to God
1. Davis, *No Falling Words,* p.200.
2. James Montgomery Boice, *Philippians,* Ministry Resources Library, 1971, p.198.

A wide range of excellent books on spiritual subjects is available from Evangelical Press. Please write to us for your free catalogue or contact us by e-mail.

Evangelical Press
Grange Close, Faverdale North Industrial Estate, Darlington, Co. Durham, DL3 0PH, England

Evangelical Press USA
P. O. Box 84, Auburn, MA 01501, USA

e-mail: sales@evangelical-press.org

web: www.evangelical-press.org